EMMAUS

the way of faith

STAGE 2: NURTURE

EMMAUS

the way of faith

STAGE 2: NURTURE

a 15-session course for exploring the Christian faith

Stephen Cottrell, Steven Croft,

John Finney, Felicity Lawson and Robert Warren

Second edition

 CHURCH HOUSE PUBLISHING

Church House Publishing
Church House
Great Smith Street
London SW1P 3NZ

ISBN 0 7151 4994 6

Second edition published 2003 by
Church House Publishing.

First edition published 1996 by
The National Society/Church House Publishing
and The Bible Society.

Tel: 020 7898 1594;
Fax: 020 7898 1449;
Email: copyright@c-of-e.org.uk.

CD-ROM created by Ambit New Media
www.ambitnewmedia.com

Cover design by Church House Publishing
Cover photograph copyright © Getty Images

Printed in England by Biddles Ltd,
Guildford and King's Lynn

Contents

Part 3   Living the Christian life

Part 4   Additional resources

CD-ROM contents

* Indicates material not in main text of book and supplied separately.

■ *all 15 members' handouts and supplementary handouts in separate files as designed and as simple text;*

■ *questions for buzz groups to be printed out in large font;*

■ *illustrative material for use in posters/adapting handouts, etc.;*

■ *twelve handouts used for introducing the idea of* Emmaus *to churches;* *

■ *three PowerPoint presentations (which can also be adapted into OHP slides) for introducing the idea of* Emmaus *to churches;* *

■ *'Resources for worship and prayer' new material for this edition;*

■ *'Celebrations on the way' from the first edition;* *

■ *Baptism, Confirmation and Affirmation of Baptismal Faith from* Common Worship: Initiation Services;

■ Emmaus *Resources Catalogue;*

■ *Links to the* Emmaus *web site;*

■ *Help page.*

Acknowledgements

Thank you!

The authors would like to say a big thank you to the many lay people and clergy who have given us feedback down the years on how the *Emmaus* Nurture course has been used in your own situation. We always find the stories very encouraging and keep on being amazed at the way God is using the material and at the variety and creativity of the ideas tried out by many different people. We would particularly like to thank Charles Freebury and Fran Wakefield, who each gave us a list of different suggestions for this edition, and the whole team at Church House Publishing, especially to Tracey Messenger and Sheridan James, who have worked closely with the authors for the last six years.

The authors and publisher gratefully acknowledge permission to reproduce copyright material in this book. Every effort has been made to trace and contact copyright holders. If there are any inadvertent omissions, we apologize to those concerned and undertake to include suitable acknowledgements in all future editions.

The Scripture quotations contained herein are from *The New Revised Standard Version of the Bible*, copyright © 1989 by the Division of Christian Education of the National Council of the Churches of Christ in the USA and are used by permission. All rights reserved.

Extracts from *Common Worship: Initiation Services* (Church House Publishing, 1998), *Common Worship: Services and Prayers for the Church of England* (Church House Publishing, 2000) and *Common Worship: Daily Prayer* (Preliminary edition, Church House Publishing, 2002) are copyright © The Archbishops' Council 1998, 2000, 2002 and are reproduced by permission.

Material from 'Rites on the Way: Work in Progress' (GS Misc 530) is copyright © The Archbishops' Council 1998 and adapted by permission.

Introduction

The Christian life is a journey. One of the most important stages on the journey is when a person who is an interested enquirer begins to learn about the faith in company with other enquirers and established Christians. The *Emmaus* nurture material is a course for such groups to follow. The course was developed in an Anglican parish in the north of England and was tried and tested in a large number of churches over seven years before it was published as part of the *Emmaus* material. Over 8,000 copies of the first edition of the course were sold. The course has now been revised for the second edition, taking into account comments and feedback from a wide range of people. Details of how the course has been revised from the first edition can be found on pages xviii–ix.

The course lasts for 15 sessions in its full form with the suggestion of a guest evening and meal together at the end. Each session is self-contained and is designed to fit into a single evening. However, you can reduce the length of the course by missing out some of the later sessions; lengthen it by adding your own material or spreading some sessions over two weeks; include a day or a weekend away; or use the different parts of the course at different times over the year. There is a certain logical order to the sessions, and the notes in the leaders' guides are written as if the sessions are being taken in order, one per week; but you may want to change them around. You may also want to use the material as a basis for three short courses instead of one of 15 sessions. The three parts can be used in a different order if you think that will work better.

The 15 sessions are:

Part 1: What Christians believe

1   *Believing in God*

2   *We need God in our lives*

3   *The life and ministry of Jesus*

4   *The death and resurrection of Jesus*

5   *The Holy Spirit*

6   *Becoming a Christian*

Part 2: How Christians grow

7   *Learning to pray*

8   *Reading the Bible*

9   *Belonging to the Church*

10   *Sharing Holy Communion*

Part 3: Living the Christian life

11   *Living God's way*

12   *Serving the Lord*

13   *Your money and your life*

14   *Learning to love*

15   *Sharing the faith.*

The numbers for the sessions are used in the leaders' guide sections of this book for ease of reference, but they are not reproduced on the members' handouts, to enable groups to vary the order.

The course is designed to help someone move on from knowing nothing about the Christian faith to becoming established as a new Christian in the life of the Church. You won't need a lot of resources in order to run a group: just a room, a couple of leaders and copies of the members' handouts for each person. It is something every church can provide at least once a year for people you come into contact with who are interested in exploring the Christian faith. All over the country adults are coming to faith through groups like this where the faith is explored and taught and relationships deepened.

The Nurture course and the *Emmaus* material

Emmaus: The Way of Faith provides books and material to help churches walk alongside those who are making the journey of faith. The material is in three parts: contact, nurture and growth. The books fit together in a series like this:

Full details of all the *Emmaus* books can be found at the back of this book. We have provided a CD-ROM with this second edition of the nurture material, containing the text of all the members' handouts (which you can use as the basis of your own adaptation of the material) and other useful material.

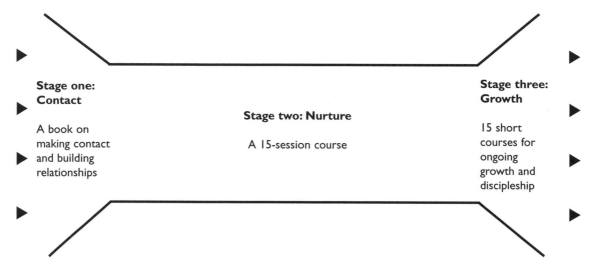

Stage one: Contact

A book on making contact and building relationships

Stage two: Nurture

A 15-session course

Stage three: Growth

15 short courses for ongoing growth and discipleship

The Emmaus road story – three elements in a journey to faith

The approach taken to evangelism throughout *Emmaus: The Way of Faith* draws on the insights of the story of the walk to Emmaus told in Luke 24. The story is about conversion: at the beginning, Cleopas and his companion are walking in the wrong direction, away from the community of disciples at Jerusalem who are at the heart of Luke's story here and in the early part of Acts. In order for them to be turned round (which is what it means to be converted) three things are important.

- *The first is that they are established in relationship and community with Jesus through listening and companionship on the road. This establishing of relationship and community is a vital part of the life of a nurture course. The group exercises in the material are designed to help this happen but much more important are the time and availability of the group leaders to offer welcome and friendship.*

- *The second is that they receive clear teaching in the Christian faith through Jesus' exposition of the Scriptures. This too is a vital part of what is happening in a nurture group. This material helps to give a shape to that teaching but the leaders themselves must make it live and enable the group to learn.*

- *The third and vital element is that the two disciples encounter the risen Christ – in this story through the breaking of the bread. In any journey to faith there is a meeting with God. This will happen and be experienced in an infinite variety of ways in private prayer and public worship.*

Planning for groups – some questions and answers

The best groups for evangelism and nurture are planned well in advance: it may take at least three months to plan and prepare for your first group of this kind and to gather the group together. Planning is an exercise of faith. Don't wait until you have twelve enquirers in the church before you begin to think about how to help them move on. Begin to prepare for the group with prayer and in faith that God will then bring you into contact with the people at the right time. The person or team planning the group will need to work through the following questions. You can find a copy of these questions in a 'think through' sheet on the CD-ROM.

Who will come?

The course is best offered to three groups of people: enquirers, new Christians and established members of the church who feel they would be helped by a 'refresher' in the basics of the faith. You will need to give particular thought to how you will come into contact as a church with interested enquirers who are at present outside the church family. The contact section of *Emmaus* should be of help here.

The group needs to be of a certain size in order to give an experience of community and to build relationships.

- *Six is a good minimum number for a group, although smaller groups can work in certain circumstances.*

- *You will find you can work as a single group with up to about ten people, breaking down into informal buzz groups for sharing and discussion.*

- *With a group of more than ten it will normally be better to break down into huddles of four or five, including a co-leader. These huddles will be the same each week so relationships can grow. In this larger group the input can be given to the whole group, but sharing and discussion should be huddle based.*

Who will lead?

You will need at least one leader who is confident enough in their Christian faith to give teaching input each week, answer the different questions an enquirer will ask and oversee the life of the group. According to Paul, laying the foundations of the Christian faith is the job of the 'master builders' in the Church (1 Corinthians 3.10). This will often be the priest, vicar or minister but may be suitably gifted and trained lay ministers. This is the place where any local church should deploy its very best teachers and leaders, whether clergy or lay. Like any task or ministry, people will get better at doing it with practice. Ideally the same leader(s) should be given the chance to specialize in this ministry and to lead a number of different groups over a period of years.

If the vicar or minister is not leading the group then he or she will need to be in close touch with the leaders from week to week throughout the preparation period and the life of the group itself to offer coaching, guidance and support.

As well as the leader(s) who give the main teaching input, the group will also need co-leaders who will be involved in getting to know those who come; praying for them and sometimes with them; leading buzz groups or huddles. We recommend a minimum of one leader and two co-leaders for even the smallest of groups with additional co-leaders for every four group members. Co-leaders should be confident in their own Christian faith but will not need to be able to teach or speak in front of the whole gathering.

When and where?

Most groups will take place in the evening with some in the daytime, possibly with a crèche provided. A weekly pattern of meetings is best because a group meeting once a fortnight will take much longer to get to know each other. Each session should last from 90 minutes to two hours, including coffee. Starting times are best fixed locally.

It is important to find a meeting place that is easily accessible and where people will feel comfortable. Some churches will have central facilities that are suitable; others will need to use people's homes (which may restrict the size of the group). People are often more at ease in a neutral venue than in someone else's house. For a group of this kind, which will involve some kind of worship and prayer, it is better to be in the Christian environment of church premises or a Christian home than in a pub or other semi-public meeting place (which are good for some of the enquirers' groups suggested in the contact section).

How will the wider church be involved?

A group like this should be seen as a central part of the ministry of the whole congregation towards enquirers and new Christians and not as the activity of an isolated group. Therefore the setting up of the group needs to be agreed and owned by the PCC (or equivalent church council) and the whole church community. Prayer support for the work is essential. The life of the group should feature regularly in intercessions in public worship and in private prayer.

Because coming to the Christian faith is best seen as an accompanied journey, many churches will also find it helpful, if not essential, to include sponsors in the week-to-week meetings of such groups. Every enquirer can be sponsored and supported by an established church member. Being a sponsor may involve a liturgical role (see below); regular prayer for the enquirer; coming to the group meetings together; and a wider ministry of befriending (see the section on sponsors on page 101 for more detail here).

What is the link with liturgy?

Different churches will want to link what is happening in the group with the public worship of the congregation in different ways. For some churches it will be enough that those who are part of the group and who come to faith in Christ express that commitment at the right time in a service of baptism, confirmation or the renewal of baptismal vows. However, it is often helpful to mark other points on the journey and the life of the group by a special service with the whole congregation. Suggestions for these Services of Welcome on the way, with ideas on how to use them, can be found at the end of this leaders' guide.

What will you call the course?

It may be helpful to think of your own name for the group in your church. It should be a name that means something to those outside the faith. We do not necessarily recommend using *Emmaus – the Nurture course*.

How will the group be gathered together?

You will need some good, simple, attractive publicity. Some resources are included on the CD-ROM to help with this. The course will need to be announced in church and in magazines and bulletins. However, the group will only be gathered together through personal invitations to those you would like to come. In issuing invitations to people try to bear the following points in mind:

- *The person giving the invitation should already have a relationship with the enquirer.*

- *Always give people the chance to say 'no' or 'not yet' or time to think about it and then come back to you.*

- *Try to dispel people's fears. Explain exactly what will happen at the meetings; that they will not be expected to speak aloud in front of the whole group (other than in the introductory session); that they will not be made to feel embarrassed in any way.*

- *Explain the need for a course of this kind and length. Most people need to learn about Christianity as adults in an adult way. That takes time. Think about the time it takes to learn to drive or learn a language or skill at evening classes.*

- *There may be practical obstacles such as transport or the need for a babysitter. Can the wider church provide help here?*

- *Never pressure anyone into coming to a group of this kind. It is far better to have a small group of people who really want to be there than a large number who are uncommitted.*

- *If the person making the invitation is not also the leader of the group then the group leaders will need to visit or speak to every person who is coming in the two weeks before the first meeting.*

One very helpful element in drawing the group together is to arrange a church 'welcome evening' a few weeks before you are due to begin. All kinds of contacts from baptisms, weddings, funerals or family services, and friends of church members can be invited to a simple supper and a short presentation about the Christian faith and the next *Emmaus* nurture group. Often people will come to one evening where they will not, initially, commit themselves to 15 weeks. Once the groups are up and running a 'welcome evening' for the next course can be hosted and arranged by members of the previous group.

What will happen after the group ends?

You will need to have some ideas for this before the first meeting. People will need to go on learning and growing in their faith after the nurture group comes to an end. The best way is through some ongoing small group in the life of the church. *Emmaus* provides material for groups to use, which is linked in with the Nurture course and is in a similar style, in four books of growth material. Often it helps to keep the group together after the course ends, possibly with two of the co-leaders sharing the task of coordinating the life of this new community. For more help in setting up groups and courses see the *Introduction* to the *Emmaus* course and the booklet, *Leading an Emmaus Group*. You will also need to have some idea about the right timing of the next nurture group. Will it be next term? In six months' time? Next year? Or will you need another group to begin before this one ends?

Preparing for and leading the meetings

There is specific advice and help for each session in this leaders' guide. You will need to plan in advance how you are going to cover the material, the dates you are going to meet, and so on. It may also help you to do some preparation and thinking in the following areas before the group begins meeting.

An outline meeting

In any one evening you will need to mix and match a number of different elements to provide a good learning and group-building experience for those who come. Eight possible elements in a meeting are:

- *People's stories*

- *Exercises*

- *Buzz groups*

- *Teaching input*

- *Plenary discussions and question times*

- *Bible study*

- *Video*

- *Coffee and chat.*

Some of these elements will be present each time (buzz groups, teaching input, plenary discussion and coffee). Others will be used in some meetings but not others. The outline sessions here give a suggested order that varies from week to week. Feel free to adapt these to what works best in your own situation.

Giving teaching input

Groups of this kind need good, clear input about the basics of the Christian faith. You will find that the amount of input needed decreases as the group grows together and is able to discuss more. Some guide to the content and structure of the input is given in the leaders' guide to each session.

When preparing and giving input do some background reading on the subject. Have a clear structure for what you say. Illustrate it as fully as possible. Do not speak for too long. Two shorter sections of teaching are usually better than one long one. If this is the first time you have done something of this kind, ask your co-leaders to give constructive encouragement and feedback each week about what went well and what could be improved.

Using more structured huddles

The outlines given here assume a group of around ten people using informal buzz groups, which will change from week to week. With a larger group it is better to use structured huddles of four to five people for some of the time each week as well as occasional buzz groups. If you are using huddles you may need to adapt the material so that the teaching input is more concentrated near the beginning of the meeting (after the opening exercise) and group exercise and discussion are together at the end.

The way groups work

One of your aims should be that the group of strangers who gather on the first evening of the course will become friends by the end. The quality of fellowship in the group will grow only slowly at first (probably up until about the tenth week). After that it will normally deepen in a measurable way from week to week. That is one of the reasons longer courses are more valuable. The way people move from being strangers to being friends is by telling their stories to one another. There is opportunity for this to happen all through the nurture stage but especially in the early weeks.

Prayer together

Ideally this too should grow and deepen as the course develops; as people grow in their Christian faith and as they get to know each other. There is a need for greater sensitivity here than in any other aspect of leading the meetings. Every group is different, even within the same church. Suggestions for prayer and worship are given in the outlines but you need to discard or adapt these to your own situation.

The course as written suggests simply a brief opening prayer said by the leader and a brief spoken prayer to close for the first six sessions. From that point on other ideas are introduced, including singing together, meditation on Scripture passages, open extemporary prayer, etc. Session 10, on Holy Communion, can be a complete act of worship in itself. Other ideas and exercises for prayer can be borrowed from other material and from the growth section of *Emmaus*.

Contact outside the group meetings

The course assumes that the leaders and co-leaders will be in contact with group members outside the group meetings through conversations in church, telephone calls and visiting. It is particularly important to have personal contact and conversation at the following points of the course:

- *in the first fortnight to check on how things are going;*

- *a fairly in-depth individual conversation in the weeks after Session 6 for discussion about individual commitment to Christ and possibly for prayer;*

- *in the final two to three weeks to discuss how people will go on growing;*

- *in preparation for any liturgical events during or after the course (baptism, confirmation, first confession, etc.).*

Wherever possible, sponsors should undertake or be involved in these points of contact. Be aware that particular sessions of the course may raise particular pastoral issues for some group members that will need to be talked and prayed through outside the meetings themselves.

One of the most common areas where churches have underestimated the commitment involved in offering an *Emmaus* nurture group is the time needed for quality conversations and meetings with group members. One of the disadvantages in offering groups for large numbers of people within the congregation is that the leaders become so stretched simply running the meetings that there is no time available for these vital pastoral encounters. It is generally better to undertake the work of Christian nurture thoroughly with a small number of people than in a superficial way with a large number.

The Gospel of Luke

The *Emmaus* Nurture course focuses on the Gospel of Luke as a way of introducing members of the group to Scripture. In the first six weeks of the course, we suggest that group members engage with the Gospel for themselves. Most of the key passages used in the different studies on the course are drawn from Luke's Gospel, including the parables of the two sons (Session 2); the sower (Session 7); and the Good Samaritan (Session 11). Session 3 contains a survey of the first part of the Gospel; Session 4 focuses on Luke's story of the passion and resurrection and Session 15 draws on the story of the Emmaus road.

Key texts

The Church of England report *On the Way* identifies four key texts that should be adopted as integral to a person's formation: the Lord's Prayer, the Apostles' Creed, the Summary of the Law and the Beatitudes (paragraph 6.11.2). Although this is an Anglican document, the texts themselves belong to all Christians and Churches. We have therefore incorporated the handing over of these key texts in this second edition of the *Emmaus* Nurture course in the following sessions:

The Apostles' Creed	6.	Becoming a Christian
The Lord's Prayer	7.	Learning to Pray
The Summary of the Law	11.	Living God's Way
The Beatitudes	15.	Sharing the Faith

Additional liturgical resources for use at this point can be found on the CD-ROM.

Travelling well

In some groups, a handbook to run alongside the course will not be appropriate: people may not be able to read or may be put off the group by being offered reading to do at home. In other situations, some background reading for group members may well be helpful. *Travelling Well* (particularly parts 2 and 3) by Stephen Cottrell and Steven Croft, makes a good handbook for members of an *Emmaus* Nurture course. There are chapters that correspond to many of the sessions of the course from Session 6 onwards. These are referred to in the leaders' guide and summarized below:

Emmaus **Nurture course**		*Travelling Well*	
6.	Becoming a Christian	1.	Beginning the way
7.	Learning to pray	3.	Learning to pray
8.	Reading the Bible	4.	Exploring the Scriptures
9.	Belonging to the Church	6.	Travelling together
10.	Sharing Holy Communion	5.	Food for the journey
11.	Living God's way	7.	Seeking the kingdom
12.	Serving the Lord	9.	Serving God
13.	Your money and your life	8.	Faith in daily life
14.	Learning to love	2.	Being changed
15.	Sharing the faith	10.	Christian witness

There are two further chapters in *Travelling Well* that can be used after the course ends or as the basis of two additional sessions:

11. *In times of difficulty*

12. *Christian hope.*

As well as a short chapter on each subject, *Travelling Well* contains readings and prayers on each theme and a short order for daily prayer.

Time away

The *Emmaus* material does not contain a specific outline for a day retreat or weekend away focusing on response to God, partly for practical and financial reasons to make the course easier to run and to take part in. However, it is certainly possible to adapt the material to include a weekend retreat or a day away: undoubtedly such an experience will add to the group's experience of relationship, community and learning. The day retreat or residential could come at any point after the first five or six weeks of the course: people need to feel confident enough in other members of the group to be able to get the most from the additional experience. Sessions 5 and 6 would work well as the theme of a day conference (if you shuffle the order of the sessions). Alternatively, you could hold a day on prayer or Holy Communion. If you need additional material for a weekend event, you may want to draw on the appropriate *Emmaus* growth material.

Meals together

In order to keep things simple both for the organizers and for the group members, we have not included the suggestion that the group eats together each week. However, meals together in an appropriate way are undoubtedly a good and deeply Christian way of forming community and relationships. As a minimum, you may want to include a simple bring and share supper after each major section of the *Emmaus* nurture course (after Sessions 6, 10 and 15).

Support for the leaders

Leading a nurture group is a tremendous privilege and opportunity for ministry. It is also demanding in terms of preparation time, the meetings themselves and caring for group members. As a team of leaders, give some advanced thought and preparation to how you will support and care for one another during this period and how you will be supported, encouraged, prayed for and cared for by the wider church family.

Resources for leaders

You will need copies of this *Nurture* book for each of the co-leaders. The members' handouts for each week will have to be photocopied in advance. Permission is given to photocopy the members' handouts for your group and to adapt the material on the CD-ROM. In most churches it will be best to give out the handouts one week at a time. You may want to supply a plastic wallet or ring-binder to each group member. Alternatively, use the masters to produce your own handbook for members – photocopied and spiral bound by a local copy shop. In addition it may be helpful to have individual copies of Luke's Gospel to give to course members (for Sessions 2, 3, 4); and a set of Bibles with common page numbers (for Session 5 onwards). The CD-ROM also contains a number of resources used for introducing the concept of *Emmaus* to church meetings and for training leaders. These resources include both handouts and PowerPoint presentations (which can be adapted into OHP slides).

Most of the sessions refer to optional video resources (the film *Jesus of Nazareth*, for example), which you may be able to buy or borrow. In preparing the teaching input you will need to read up on various subjects. Some ideas for this reading are given in the leaders' guide to each session. See the section 'Other resources referred to in the text' on page 117 for a full list of films quoted. You will also find a full list of books referred to in the text, with publication details, in the 'Bibliography and further reading' section on pages 115–116.

One-to-one links

Sometimes it is not possible for someone to come to a nurture group. You may not have the resources within your church to get one going at first. In a very small church there may not be enough enquirers to form even a small group. Someone may not be able to come at a time your group meets because of work or family commitments or for health reasons. Or a person may become a Christian through the life of an ongoing house group. It may be better for them (and the group) that they continue to be nurtured in that group than come to a special nurture course.

In any of these circumstances the *Emmaus* nurture material can be adapted and used one to one. You will need to find someone who has been a Christian for several years, preferably of the same sex and social background, to be the 'senior partner' in the link. Both members of the partnership will need a set of handouts. The pair should then aim to meet together for an hour or so every fortnight to go through the material and discuss any questions that may arise. At the growth stage, the link could develop into a less frequent ongoing meeting, perhaps using some of the *Emmaus* growth material or the series of Bible Resources.

Keeping on keeping on

Research and experience both suggest that perseverance is absolutely essential in any church offering a group or course of this kind. The first time you offer the course, numbers may be quite large but, typically, there may only be two or three people who are on the edge of the church as enquirers. The rest of the group may well be interested members of the congregation who are looking to refresh their understanding of Christian faith or who are simply curious about a new venture. It is very important in this kind of group that the material is pitched at the level of the enquirers rather than the established Christians. The second time you offer the course, numbers are normally even lower: some enquirers but not as many established Christians. It is at this point that many churches give up on the whole project. However, experience suggests that if a church perseveres and offers a course a third, fourth and fifth time then it becomes well established, is able to attract consistently both enquirers and those on the edge of Christian faith, and significant numbers of people come to faith and grow in faith.

General reading

Emmaus Introduction and *Contact*

Leading an Emmaus Group

On the Way: towards an integrated approach to Christian Initiation

John Finney, *Finding Faith Today: how does it happen?*

What's new in the second edition?

General comments

Inclusive language has been used throughout the Nurture course in the second edition. We have used a standard text of the Bible throughout *Emmaus* (the NRSV) and quotations are from this version.

We have taken the opportunity of the second edition to harmonize the course material with the Church of England's *Common Worship* material in the one or two places where that is necessary. However, it remains very easy to adapt the handouts to the needs of different churches. We have also provided more extensive background reading for leaders (which has been requested) and more explicit links with other *Emmaus* materials. You will also find a wider range of suggestions for using video as appropriate. *Travelling Well*, by Stephen Cottrell and Steven Croft, is recommended as an optional link book for course members from Session 6 onwards. We have made greater use of the Gospel of Luke in the second half of the course, introducing additional material from the Gospel at a number of points.

The material in the members' handouts has been reduced from the first edition in order to produce a handout that can be copied onto two sides of A4 paper rather than three or four sides. The amount of content for group members is very similar to the first edition: the handouts are smaller because we have removed the group exercises to the leaders' guide and have designed the handouts in a different way. We have also removed the page numbers from the members' handouts to help churches who want to tackle the sessions in a different order or provide extra material at some points. In some cases you may need to write out the questions on a flip chart or copy the questions onto reusable cards. You will also find them on the CD-ROM. The members' handouts have been interspersed with the leaders' guide in this edition instead of being grouped together at the end of the book.

Additional material has been included in the Introduction to the course on the *Emmaus* series of materials, time away and meals together. We have also included in this edition the four key texts identified in the report *On the Way* as important in Christian initiation (see p. xv).

Particular sessions

In Session 2 there is an increased emphasis on God the Father and on sin affecting the whole of creation, not simply individual lives. The section on death in the first edition ('The fear of the future') has been changed to 'Our longing for eternity'.

Session 3 now focuses on the life and ministry of Jesus and Session 4 on Jesus' death and resurrection. A common response to the first edition was that it was difficult to do justice to all the material in the old Session 3, so this session has been substantially rewritten using a smaller number of texts from the first part of Luke's Gospel but giving opportunity to explore them in more depth. There is a greater emphasis on the incarnation, the proclamation of the kingdom and on Jesus bringing salvation to the whole of creation to complement the emphasis on forgiveness and new life for individuals. The C. S. Lewis quotation about the claims of Jesus has been changed to one by Michael Ramsey.

Session 4 has been rewritten around the death and resurrection of Jesus. A wider group of images of salvation has been used for reflection on the meaning of the cross. A reading from *The Pilgrim's Progress* has been provided as an optional ending to this session.

Session 5 is substantially the same except that we have included material on the ascension of Jesus (missing from the first edition). The questions and answers from the first edition have been transferred to an optional supplementary handout.

Session 6 has been rewritten. Additional material has been provided in the leaders' guide on when to hold this session in the course and how to link it with public acts of commitment and dedication to Christ. In general we have strengthened the link between this session and baptism through including material on baptism in the teaching element of the session. The Apostles' Creed has been used as the first key text and as a summary for the first six sessions of the course, alongside a briefer summary of the gospel. Discerning readers might detect a greater emphasis upon God's gracious gift. A supplementary handout is provided with prayers in response to God's grace. The material on individual interviews after this session remains substantially the same.

Session 7, 'Learning to pray', has given a more central place to the Lord's Prayer. Session 8 on the Scriptures is only lightly revised. In Session 9, the section on biblical images of the Church has been sharpened to focus on the Church in relation to God, herself, the world and to time. The material on baptism in this session has been moved to Sessions 6 and 11. The material in Session 10 is substantially the same.

Session 11 has been rewritten. The initial discussion of the Ten Commandments flows into a discussion of Jesus' Summary of the Law. This is followed (as in the Gospel of Luke) by a study of the parable of the Good Samaritan as a third significant passage from the Gospel for Part 3. The example situations have moved forward in the session. The material on growing in grace in the Christian life in this session has been reduced to make space for these additions. The martial imagery of the first edition has been reduced (in line with the developments in Initiation services in many of the Churches).

Session 12 on ministry has been developed. The (often powerful) opening exercise is retained but is now followed by a section linking Christian service and ministry explicitly to baptism. We have included a section on the five marks of mission to set the understanding of ministry within a broad context of mission rather than a narrow context of maintaining the church. This session and the next place an increased emphasis on the truth that ministry is often exercised outside the congregation.

Session 13 on 'Your money and your life' has also been developed by introducing material on vocation and extending the thinking about work. The Bible study is now on attitudes to money generally (not just the money we give away) and uses only passages from Luke's Gospel. The material on stewardship, giving and church finance is retained. Session 14 on 'Learning to love' has been only lightly revised.

Session 15 has been rewritten around two Bible passages. The different threads in Part 3 of the course are drawn together in a study of the Beatitudes from Matthew's Gospel. The material on sharing your faith is now covered largely through a study of the Emmaus road story from Luke 24.

The material on sponsors is largely unchanged from the first edition. We have completely re-written the Rites on the Way in the first edition to harmonize the material in *Emmaus* with the recent work of the Church of England liturgical commission (which is itself drawing on a range of ecumenical sources). The end material contains a full bibliography of all the works cited in earlier sections.

Key to the icons used in the leaders' notes and members' handouts

 Material available to print out from the CD-ROM

 Suggestions for multi-media resources

 Introduction to the session

 Example timings for the session

 Testimony

 Material for reflection

 Buzz groups

 Summary of the session

 Question time

 Suggestions for prayer

 Further reading for leaders

 Key text

part 01]

What Christians believe

Believing in God

Introduction

The first session of a nurture group is never an easy one to lead as a group of strangers comes together for the first time. You may not know exactly who is coming. The people attending will probably be even more apprehensive and nervous than you are yourself. Particular preparation and prayer are needed.

Make sure that you yourself and the co-leaders are 'on site' at least 30 minutes before the meeting is due to begin. Pray together; check through the plan for the evening; make sure everyone is aware of their responsibilities and that you have all you need. Take care how you arrange the room and make the arrangements for coffee. It is better to underestimate the number of chairs required. You should already have made arrangements for transport to the first meeting.

As people arrive the leader and co-leaders should talk with them, welcome them and begin to get to know them, making introductions between people where necessary. Good hosting is important. Some people will probably arrive quite early and others may be a few minutes late. On this occasion, a cup of tea or coffee before the meeting may help people to settle down. A small lending library of books can also provide something to look at in the room.

Getting to know you

As near to time as you can, welcome everyone, open in prayer and give a little bit of background to the group and what its purpose is. Give out the session handouts. Explain that one of the benefits of a course like this is getting to know other people as well as learning more about the Christian faith. Then begin with the opening exercise. Ask people to talk in pairs to someone they do not know and explain that you will then ask them to introduce their partner to the whole group in a few minutes' time, using the following questions as a guide. If you think it will help, write or print up the questions on a large sheet of paper that everyone can see. Every section printed in a box like the one below is available on the CD-ROM in large print as a poster. In some settings you may need to adapt the questions (such as a course offered in a prison or with people who may lack confidence).

- *Your name*

- *Your home situation*

- *Your work situation*

- *What's the best thing that has happened to you in the last year?*

- *Why have you come to this course?*

This exercise can be daunting but it is the only time in the whole course that people will be asked to speak in front of the whole group. The reason the exercise is done this way is that it is much easier for most people to introduce someone else than to talk about themselves.

Once people have found a partner and have begun talking you may need to call 'half-time' after five minutes so that the partners can change roles. Introducing everyone to the group will take time – but it is well worth it. In this exercise everyone is introduced and everyone gets over the hurdle of speaking in front of the whole group (unless you really don't think they can handle it – in which case give them an opportunity to pass). Ideally the leader or a co-leader should go first in introducing a partner, giving a pattern for others to follow.

The aim is that through the exercise people discover a little bit about each other and discover why other members of the group are there – probably for similar reasons to themselves. Remember that a key part of the group's life in the early weeks is to build trust and community.

Testimony

It can be excellent at this point to have one person sharing more personally and telling the story of his or her journey to faith. Ideally on the first night this should be the leader or one of the co-leaders. Especially if the group is being led by the vicar or minister, group members need to know how the leader has come to be a Christian, that it was a gradual process over time (if it was) and that you are still learning. You may need to practise this part of your input beforehand with one of the co-leaders. It should not take more than about five minutes.

Introduction to the course and ground rules

Explain a little more about the group (depending on the way you intend it to run). If you are using it in the normal form, explain that the course will last for 15 sessions; that it is divided into three main sections; that people come for different reasons; that the course is run regularly in your church (or that this is the first of a regular series).

Introduce Part 1 (the first six sessions) by explaining that you will be looking at the basics of what Christians believe about God; about our need for him; about Jesus and the Holy Spirit; and ending the first part by answering the question: 'What is a Christian?' Explain also that you will be addressing everyone in the first section of the course as if they are all interested enquirers (even though you know some have been Christians for many years).

It helps to take a few moments to go over some ground rules for the group. The ground rules we recommend are:

■   *Please make a commitment to be here each week (or let us know if you cannot come).*

■   *Please be punctual.*

■   *Please be honest and real in everything you say and ask the questions that are in your minds.*

Explain, finally, that each week there will be plenty of opportunities to ask questions about any aspect of the Christian faith.

A break for buzz groups . . .

By this time people may have been listening for some time. Ask them to break into groups of two or three and discuss the following question.

If someone were to come up to you in the street tomorrow and ask you whether you believe in God and why, what would you say?

Again, it may help to write up the question on a large sheet of paper.

Is God really there?

Pick up from the buzz groups by asking people to share their answers to the question, then go into a brief teaching input based on the handout, which aims to show:

■   *that the question of whether or not God exists is very important;*

■   *that the question of God's existence is not a matter of opinion but of evidence.*

Experience suggests that some groups may need to spend quite a bit of time on this question but, for the majority, the existence of God will be a 'given' and there may be a sense that you are starting too far back.

Buzz groups

In a small group of three or four, ask people to talk about their own belief in God around one or two of the following questions.

■   *Do you identify with these two things people often say?*

■   *Has your faith in God been constant through your life or has it changed?*

■   *Why do you think some people find it hard to believe in God?*

■   *What evidence can you think of that points to his existence?*

If you used the last exercise the group may not be quite ready to stop here. Use your own judgement at the time. It may be better to cover the section 'Seeing God in creation' before breaking for discussion.

'I believe in God'

1   Seeing God in creation

Again a session of teaching input based on the headings on the sheet. Because we live in such an artificial world, many people are out of touch with just how wonderful the universe is. You will need to find some way of communicating this through words, video, slides or pictures. A flip chart may be helpful to write down all the things people find amazing about the universe. Once you have explored the wonder of the universe, ask the three questions listed.

2   Seeing God in yourself

As important as the previous question. People may not be as comfortable at sharing 'wonderful things' about themselves.

Question time

After the input (with or without flip chart) again ask people to break into small groups and discuss what they make of all that and what questions it raises. It is much easier, generally, for people to identify questions in small groups before asking them in the larger gathering.

Then go into a general question and answer session. Be prepared for anything. When answering questions try and remember:

■ *to affirm the questioner ('that's a good question . . .');*

■ *not to argue or be defensive (God can stick up for himself);*

■ *to be honest in your answers;*

■ *to say so if you don't know the answer – offer to do some homework and to come back next week.*

Anything can be thrown at you in a question time. It really is an opportunity to depend on the Holy Spirit. Experience suggests that, if the question time really gets going, you might expect some questions on the relationship between Christian faith and science and on the interpretation of the early chapters of Genesis. Ideas are given about this in the reading material.

Knowing God for yourself

End the session with a brief epilogue based on the notes. There is a world of difference between knowing about God and knowing God.

Close the session in prayer, possibly reading Psalm 8 or playing a version of the Psalm on tape. Draw attention briefly to the Bible passages for the coming week.

Coffee

You may think you can sit back and relax over coffee. It is actually one of the most important parts of the session. Take time to talk with people as individuals. If you can, speak to each person before they leave to check they found the group OK and to uncover any anxieties. Remember that you have no idea what was going on in the buzz groups, and that someone may have been disturbed, offended or upset.

Ideally, in the week following the session, the leader and co-leaders should double-check that each person found the session useful and plans to continue with the group. It is worth saying either to the whole group or to individuals that it really does get better as people relax and get to know each other.

Reading for leaders

For more on the relationship between Christian faith and science, especially the origins of the universe, see David Wilkinson, *God, Time and Stephen Hawkins*, Monarch, 2001.

The *Emmaus* growth course on 'Growing in the Scriptures' (in *Growth Book 2: Growing as a Christian*) has a supplementary handout on the first five books of the Old Testament.

Video and multimedia material

You might find useful clips for discussion in three places:

- *science fiction material that attempts to explore the question of the wonder, extent and origins of the universe (such as the Star Wars trilogy);*

- *material from documentaries about life on earth, particularly about the detail and design in creation;*

- *sections of films or television materials that ask important questions about what it means to be human (such as a clip from the end of The Truman Show where Truman decides to leave the artificial world created for him by the television company).*

Summary and example timings

Each leader will tackle the session in their own way. Approximate timings for the session are outlined here. Remember that the length of the opening exercise will vary according to the size of the group. The overall session time should be about 90 minutes not including coffee.

	mins
Introduction: Welcome, prayer and opening exercise	15
Testimony: The leader's story	5
Introduction and ground rules	5
Buzz groups	10
Is God really there?	10
Buzz groups	5
'I believe in God'	15
Buzz groups for questions	10
Question time	10
Knowing God, and closing prayer	5
Coffee	

Believing in God

Is God really there?

Some people might say: **'It doesn't matter anyway.'**

But this is the most important question in the whole universe.

The answer you give will affect your whole life.

Either God is there – or God isn't. There's no half way.

If God is there, then there is meaning and purpose in life. God calls us into friendship and into a Christian way of life. There is a life beyond this life.

If God is not there, then the whole meaning of life is changed. You have to find that meaning from within yourself. You can please yourself if you like. There is no joy or pleasure or hope greater than you have now – this is all life offers.

Others may say: **'It's just a matter of opinion.'**

People think this way because it is the way they want to think.

It's really much more comfortable. It gets you off the hook.

Once you admit that God may be there, life becomes much more challenging. You need to look further at what God is like and at what God's purpose for your life may be.

Belief in the God who made heaven and earth is not a matter of opinion. Belief in God is a matter of evidence.

When you begin to look, there is a great deal of evidence. And it all points one way . . .

'I believe in God'

There are many different ways to sum up the evidence that points to God's existence. This is one way.

1   Seeing God in creation

Share together the things you find the most amazing about creation and the natural world. You may like to use Psalm 8 as a starting point.

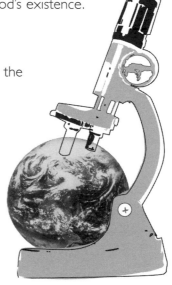

Then ask these questions:

■   *The universe had a beginning. Who began it?*

■   *The universe has order and beauty. Who arranged it?*

■   *The universe shows evidence of design. Who is the designer?*

All the evidence of our senses and of the sciences points us to God who created the heavens and the earth.

2   Seeing God in yourself

Again, share together the things you find that are wonderful about yourself and about people in general.

Then ask these questions:

■   *Everyone has a sense of right and wrong – a conscience. This is true the whole world over. Who put it there?*

■   *All men and women have an inbuilt need to worship someone or something. Why is that need to worship there?*

■   *All people long to experience love. It can be the most powerful force in our lives. Where did it come from?*

3   Knowing God for yourself

Christians believe that God made the universe. We believe that humankind is special within God's creation. And we believe that God has shown us what he is like, through the Bible and in Jesus Christ.

God, the maker of heaven and earth, calls us into friendship through Jesus. And knowing God changes our whole lives.

Psalm 8

O Lord, our Sovereign, how majestic is your name in all the earth!
You have set your glory above the heavens.
Out of the mouths of babes and infants you have founded a bulwark because
of your foes, to silence the enemy and the avenger.

When I look at your heavens, the work of your fingers, the moon and the stars that
you have established;
what are human beings that you are mindful of them,
mortals that you care for them?

Yet you have made them a little lower than God,
and crowned them with glory and honour.
You have given them dominion over the works of your hands;
you have put all things under their feet,
all sheep and oxen, and also the beasts of the field,
the birds of the air, and the fish of the sea,
whatever passes along the paths of the seas.

O Lord, our Sovereign,
how majestic is your name in all the earth.

For reflection

Take time to thank God this week for the wonder of creation – of the universe and of humankind. Ask for God's grace and help as you continue your journey of faith.

Emmaus Nurture course handout: Believing in God

We need God in our lives

Introduction

This is potentially one of the most important and helpful sessions in the whole course. It is when people really begin to think about God and their own lives and where they are in relation to him. Be careful in your own preparation both in practical ways and in prayer.

Sharing your story

As near to the start time as possible, welcome the group and open in prayer. Make a special mention of anyone who is there for the first time. It is normally fine for anyone to join the group up to the fourth session of the course while the group is still gelling together. Introduce the opening exercise, which asks people to talk about their own home background. It is best if people form small clusters for the buzz groups just with the people on either side of them. The groups should not be larger than four people, otherwise the sharing will take too long. The exercise is meant to help people to get to know one another and to introduce the theme of the story of two sons. Some groups may find sharing at this level so early in the course a bit threatening, so you may need to adapt the questions.

In small groups share with each other your own memories of living at home and of childhood.

- *What were the best things about childhood for you?*

- *Was there anything unusual about your own childhood?*

- *At what age did you leave home? How did it feel?*

Testimony

Pick up from the buzz groups and, if you include a testimony, give a brief introduction to the person who is sharing their story. They should then speak for no more than five minutes. It may be that the group would like to ask them questions following on from what they have shared.

The story of two sons

Most people won't know the story very well (Luke 15.11-32). It is probably best if the leader or one of the co-leaders tells the parable in a lively way, and then draws out the different stages in the younger son's journey. If you have been able to obtain copies of the Gospel of Luke, then give them out at this point so that people can follow the story in the Gospel. If you have dramatic gifts, then act it out. The film *Jesus of Nazareth* contains an excellent section where Jesus tells the story in the house of Matthew the tax collector. For a supplementary handout describing different stages on the younger son's journey see *Emmaus Growth Book 1: Knowing God* on pages 16–18.

Some groups working through the nurture material contain a majority of people who have been Christians for most of their lives. Some people in the group may not be able to identify very easily with the story of the younger son and may need additional help to draw out the significance of the elder brother in the story.

After you have told the story, suggest that people take a moment to reflect on the different stages of the journey and then discuss with one or two other people where they find themselves on this inner journey. Give people permission to be at more than one stage at a time. Allow plenty of time for this sharing in buzz groups. If the group is not too large it will be well worth taking a brief report back from each of the small groups before going into the main teaching content.

To link this section with the one that follows, end the Bible study by drawing out what the parable says about the love of God. Draw out the nature of God as Father, which is found all through the Scriptures and is beautifully captured in this parable, and in the Lord's Prayer. Some Christians find the picture a difficult one because of their own experiences of fathers. Others find the concept straightforward.

How do we know that we need God?

You will need to think through in advance how often you will break for discussion during this session. You could pause for buzz groups, questions or plenary discussion after each of the sections. As you become more experienced in leading a group, you will find you can think on your feet. When people's eyes start to glaze over and they yawn, fidget and stare at the carpet, it is usually a cue for buzz groups and discussion.

The opening point is an important one: a need is a need even if it is not admitted to or recognized by the person concerned. From there go on to talk about the space in our heart, the walls that we build and our fear of the future, stopping along the way for questions and discussion.

After the section on 'The space in your heart', spend some time pooling your ideas on how people try and fill up that inner space. Be sure to mention good as well as bad things. St Augustine was a bishop in North Africa in the fourth century. The words of the prayer come at the beginning of his famous *Confessions*, which describes his conversion to Christian faith.

The second section, 'The chaos in creation', is important because all of us need to realize that our longing to be restored to God is not simply a longing to be plucked out of the world as individuals (so that we are OK no matter what happens to society around us). It is, at its best, a longing for God's salvation and peace to come to the whole of creation and a cry of protest that things are so disordered at the present time.

In the section 'The walls we build' it is helpful to unpack our pride, guilt and unwillingness to change:

- *Our pride*
  We hate to admit that we are not number one. Something inside us hates to surrender, hates to worship. Pride is the root of all human sin and tragedy.

- *Our guilt*
  The wrong things we do and say and are have a serious effect on other people and on ourselves. We think that God cannot forgive us, or give us a new beginning.

- *Our unwillingness to change*
  Coming to God means change – all sorts of change. Much of the time we do not like the idea, so another part of the wall goes up.

Be prepared for different responses in different members of the group. Some will be all too conscious of their pride, their need for forgiveness and unwillingness to change. Others may find this section very challenging and react against it in different ways.

The fourth section, 'Our longing for eternity', may raise difficult questions about life and death, heaven and judgement. The questions need to be given space and time but the answers to some of them may need to be left to a later session.

People normally find all of these sections challenging and usually can identify at some point with the teaching and input given. Again, at the end of the teaching ask people to break into buzz groups to respond to what has been said and identify any questions that arise.

Question time

As for the first session, give people an opportunity to ask about anything at all that concerns them. Be prepared this week for questions about life after death: Do we believe in reincarnation? Is Christianity the only way? What about those who have never heard the gospel?

Final summary

Don't just drift out of questions and into coffee. Draw the evening together properly. Summarize what has been said and focus the message of the evening into a challenge people can take away with them and think about. It is helpful to point the group back to the picture of the father's love in the story of the two sons. Look ahead to the next session when we begin to look at Jesus. Refer people to the copies of Luke's Gospel (if you intend to use them). Explain briefly what a Gospel is and suggest people read a short section each day over the next few weeks. Close the evening with prayer and coffee time. You may want to say the Lord's Prayer and invite the group to join in without saying the words.

Reading for Leaders

Chapter 5 of *The Mystery of Salvation* entitled 'Retelling the story' is excellent background reading for this session and the session on the death and resurrection of Jesus.

Chapter 2 of *Travelling Well* deals with 'being changed' (pp. 13–25) and Chapter 12 with 'Christian hope' (pp. 121–29). Both chapters contain prayers and readings.

Henri Nouwen's book, *The Return of the Prodigal Son*, is a powerful treatment of the parable and Rembrandt's painting on the subject.

There is a great deal of material on God the Father in the *Emmaus* growth course, 'Knowing the Father' (in *Growth Book 1: Knowing God*). The growth course, 'Growing in Prayer' (in *Growth Book 2: Growing as a Christian*) is based around the Lord's Prayer.

Video and multimedia material

Pauline Books and Media (Middle Green, Slough SL3 6BS, www.pauline-uk.org) can supply posters and postcard-sized reproductions of Rembrandt's painting of the *Return of the Prodigal Son*.

The video clip of the telling of the story from *Jesus of Nazareth* is referred to above. The themes of pride, guilt, breakdown in relationships and death are commonly dealt with in films and soaps. It should not be too difficult to find clips to introduce these themes or on the chaos in creation:

clips from the latest newspaper headlines or news bulletins will be helpful. Because these are themselves serious subjects, a lighter way of introducing them will work well. *The Simpsons – Heaven and Hell* (Fox) is able to make people think and laugh at the same time on the issues surrounding death.

Summary and example timings

Again, these are just a guide. The timings here allow for one brief buzz break during the teaching input.

	mins
Sharing your story	15
Testimony	5
The story of two sons	10
Buzz groups	10
How do we know that we need God? (1)	10
Buzz groups	5
How do we know that we need God? (2) and (3)	15
Buzz groups for questions	5
Question time	10
Final summary and prayer	5
Coffee	

We need God in our lives

The story of two sons

A vital part of coming to know God is realizing how lost we are.

Jesus told a story about a man who had two sons, to teach us how we all, in some way, wander away from God's love. We rebel and we do not begin to return home until we realize our need for God again.

The story is in Luke 15.11-32.

All of us in our lives are on two journeys. There is an outer journey – which involves things like our school, work and significant relationships. There is also an inner journey – which involves our relationship with God. The story of the lost son is about our inner journey.

Where are you on your own inner journey?

- *Running away?*

- *Living far away, having a good time?*

- *Sensing your need of your heavenly Father?*

- *Turning round to come back?*

- *On your way home?*

- *In the arms of your Father?*

- *Like the elder brother – you've been a Christian so long you take it all for granted?*

- *Learning to take your place in the family?*

- *None of these or several of them?*

How easy or difficult do you find it to think of God as Father?

How do we know that we need God?

Our need for God is often well hidden – but the need for God is there in everyone.

I   The space in your heart

> O Lord, you have made us for yourself, and our hearts
> are restless until they rest in you.
>
> St Augustine

God calls us into friendship. If we don't have that relationship with God, something is missing. There is a space, an inner restlessness, in our lives.

People spend their whole lives trying to fill that space with all kinds of things. But in the end, nothing will satisfy, except the living God.

You can recognize that inner space in your own life by asking yourself these questions:

- *Do I have a sense of purpose?*

- *Do I have a sense of inner peace in my life?*

- *Do I have a longing to be loved?*

God promises to give to each one who comes home a new sense of purpose, of peace and of love.

2   The chaos in creation

All through history, men and women have longed for stability, security, peace, freedom and justice. We have only to look at the world around us to realize that these things are hard to attain. Something deep within us cries out to God for salvation not simply for ourselves but for the whole world.

3   The walls we build

Part of the mystery of being human is recognizing our capacity for harm as well as for good. The Bible says that we are sinners and we have a sinful nature.

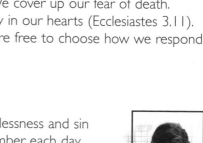

This means that, although we know that God is there, we want nothing to do with the love God offers to us. We build walls to keep God out.

We are separated and cut off from God by:

- *Our pride*
  We hate to admit that we are not number one. Something inside us hates to surrender, hates to worship. Pride is the root of all human sin and tragedy.

- *Our guilt*
  The wrong things we do and say and are have a serious effect on other people and on ourselves. We think that God cannot forgive us, or give us a new beginning.

- *Our unwillingness to change*
  Coming to God means change – all sorts of change. Much of the time we do not like the idea, so another part of the wall goes up.

4   Our longing for eternity

One day each of us will die. We don't like to think about it. We cover up our fear of death. No one wants to die. The Bible says that God has put eternity in our hearts (Ecclesiastes 3.11). Through Jesus the offer of eternal life is made to all. But we are free to choose how we respond to this offer.

For reflection

This week, think about your own need of God: your own restlessness and sin and fear. Read Psalm 51 and use the psalm as a prayer. Remember each day that God loves the world, that God loves you and is calling you home.

The life and ministry of Jesus

Introduction

In Session 1 we looked at our reasons for believing in God; in Session 2 at the truth that we need God but are separated from his love. Sessions 3 and 4 look at the way God draws us back into a relationship with himself through Jesus.

The person and character of Jesus as presented in the Gospels draw us to the love of God. As the letter to the Hebrews says, 'He is the reflection of God's glory and the exact imprint of God's very being' (Hebrews 1.3). John's Gospel calls Jesus 'the true light, which enlightens everyone' (John 1.9).

There is no better way to be introduced to Jesus than through one of the Gospels. We have chosen Luke's Gospel for the *Emmaus* Nurture course because it was written for Gentile (non-Jewish) Christians and enquirers in order to pass on the testimony of those who knew Jesus and were eyewitnesses of the events described (Luke 1.1-4). The Gospel contains a good balance between Jesus' actions and his teachings and the two are interwoven throughout. Luke seems to have used Mark's Gospel as a guide to the shape of his account of Jesus. He shares some material in common with Matthew, possibly taken from an independent source of Jesus' teaching. He also has his own sources and includes parables and events in Jesus' ministry which are found only in Luke.

The way in which you guide a nurture group through Luke's Gospel will vary according to the group's preferred style of learning. Some groups will be able to take a Gospel away with them, read it and come back together and discuss it. Others will need to be guided through the text. Other groups may consist wholly or partly of people who cannot read for themselves in a meaningful way. You will therefore need to read or retell the stories for them either by reading aloud, storytelling or watching a video. The *Jesus* video will be very helpful in this session as it is a faithful representation of the text of Luke. It may be helpful to have some copies available to lend to group members.

The shape of the session is a guide to the life and ministry of Jesus, focused around the question Jesus himself asks of Simon Peter at a key point in the Gospel: 'But who do you say that I am?' (Luke 9.20). In preparation for that question, the session looks at four different parts of Luke's testimony about Jesus, focused around four passages in the Gospels:

- *Jesus' birth (Luke 1.26-38);*

- *Jesus' ministry (Luke 4.38-44);*

- *Jesus and the forgiveness of sins (Luke 7.36-50);*

- *Who do you say I am? (Luke 9.12-26).*

For each part of the session, you may want to read the passage aloud, tell the story in your own words or watch a video clip.

Welcome and testimony

If you are using testimony this week you may want to have it right at the beginning, as the buzz group exercise is closely linked with the teaching.

Welcome thegroup, open with a short prayer and introduce the person who is speaking. This may be one of the group, one of the co-leaders, or another member of the church who has come specifically to share their story. Take care when thinking about who to ask to give a testimony to have a wide variety of different kinds of people and experiences to give a balanced picture. Alternatively, there may be someone in the group who is able to speak honestly and simply about the way in which they have received forgiveness of sins and a new beginning. This would be better at the point indicated below.

How much do you know about Jesus?

Give a brief introduction to the session and talk in a concise way about why knowing about Jesus is central to the Christian faith. Then ask people to divide into small groups to think about the questions below. Note that this is the first time people have been asked to talk in small groups about what they know. The other exercises have been asking them to talk about themselves. Give them permission to share ignorance as well as knowledge! It may help to offer to end the buzz groups quickly if there is a deafening silence in the room (there almost certainly won't be).

- *What attracts you about Jesus of Nazareth?*

- *What questions do you have about him?*

- *How much (if any) of the Gospels have you read?*

- *Has your impression of Jesus changed as you have grown older?*

Jesus' life and ministry

It will be helpful to begin by establishing that Jesus is a real figure in history and by introducing the Gospels as written to tell us about his life, ministry, death and resurrection.

For each passage, read or retell the story, give some brief teaching or exploration based on the notes on the sheet and give the group the opportunity to respond and ask questions.

Jesus' birth (Luke 1.26-38)

The story of Jesus' birth is probably the most familiar part of the Gospel accounts to those outside the Churches.

In teaching new Christians about Jesus, it is very important to give some background to his life and ministry from the Old Testament. It may be useful to tell the story of God's people, Israel, from the call of Abraham and describe their longing for a king: these longings echo the cry of men and women in every generation for stability, security from their enemies, freedom to live in peace and a just ordering of society and of creation. The person and message of Jesus address these longings and this disorder in the language of the kingdom of God. You may want to refer back to the section 'The chaos in creation' in the Session 2.

The message of salvation has, at its heart, the good news that men and women are offered forgiveness for their sins, reconciliation with God and eternal life. However, the message of salvation is also about the reordering of society and of creation through the establishing of God's kingdom, in Jesus, in every generation and, finally and completely, at the end of time.

It may be helpful to refer to the part Mary plays in the story of salvation and to the belief expressed in the creeds that Jesus is fully God and fully human.

Jesus' ministry (Luke 4.16-24 and 38-44)

Again, it is vital that Jesus' teaching and the miracles are placed in the context of the proclamation of the kingdom of God. It is also important to understand that Jesus' message was difficult and divisive and, from the very beginning of his ministry, there were those who wanted to kill him as well as those who flocked to hear him teach and witness the miracles.

There may be questions in the group around Jesus' miracles of healing and the relationship with sickness, suffering and miracles today. There will almost certainly be questions about the references to demons and deliverance in the Gospels. Again, it may be helpful to talk about the universal human longings for health (so obvious in society around us) and freedom from oppression of different kinds, including the oppression of evil.

At this point it may help to give people an opportunity to talk in groups and reflect on what has been said so far. Helpful starter questions may be:

■   *Why do you think some people were so attracted to Jesus yet others so hostile to him?*

■   *How would you have responded?*

Jesus and the forgiveness of sins (Luke 7.36-50)

This passage gives the opportunity to refer back to the material in Session 2 in the story of the two sons and the walls that we build; to discuss the way in which our past actions separate us from God and the way that Jesus offers a new beginning. The image of debts being cancelled is a powerful one and well worth exploring.

You may need to give a brief explanation here about the Pharisees, about why the woman's sins mean she is excluded from society and about the 'scandal' of Jesus being touched by the woman in this way.

Again, it may be helpful to reflect on the different responses of the woman, of the Pharisee and of those at table with Jesus (v. 49). There may be people present in the group who are able to talk about their own sense of past sins being forgiven and being welcomed back into the community of God's people.

Who do you say I am? (Luke 9.12-26)

If time is pressing, you may want to omit Luke 9.12-17 and begin the episode with the conversation about Jesus' identity.

As an introduction, remind the group of the different questions raised in the Gospel so far about who Jesus is: by the prophecies about him, by his words about himself and by his actions.

Move from a discussion of Peter's recognition of Jesus to Jesus asking the question of each of us: who do you say that I am? The quotation may be useful here. Michael Ramsey was Archbishop of Canterbury (1961–74).

Moving on to Jesus' prediction of his death is an excellent way to look ahead to the second half of Luke's Gospel and to the next session of the nurture course. You may want to end with buzz groups and a discussion based around the following question:

■   *What do you think is the cost of following Jesus today?*

The same groups can also draw out any general questions arising from the session.

Question time

The session has covered a lot of ground. It may, therefore, be helpful simply to listen to people's questions and perhaps write them down rather than answer them as a whole group. Different issues might be pursued over coffee together.

Final summary

Recap on the main points covered through the evening and anything that has been particularly important to the group. Encourage people to continue to engage with Luke's Gospel. It may be helpful to suggest that people may have different responses to Jesus and his message, just as in the Gospels. A person's first response may not be their last. End with the question Jesus asks us all: 'But who do you say I am?' Close the formal part of the group with a time of quiet and a short prayer.

Reading for leaders

The best preparation for this session is reading through Luke's Gospel for yourself, possibly with a simple commentary such as Henry Wansbrough's volume in the *People's Bible Commentary* series. See also Tom Wright, *Luke for Everyone*.

You will find more material on Jesus for this session and the next one in *Emmaus Growth Book 1: Knowing God* in the course 'Knowing Jesus'.

Chapter 4 of *The Mystery of Salvation*, 'The story of the saviour', may be a helpful guide to some of the ideas in this session. For more on the idea of the kingdom of God and the mission of Jesus see J. Andrew Kirk, *What is Mission?*, chapter 3, 'Mission in the Way of Jesus Christ'.

For an excellent and highly readable recent book on Jesus see David Day, *Pearl beyond Price*, The Archbishop of Canterbury's Lent Book for 2002.

Video and multimedia material

The film *Jesus* based on the Gospel of Luke is probably the best resource for this session.

USPG produces a very helpful set of 32 postcards with different representations of Christ in a pack entitled 'The Christ we Share'. Using this at the beginning of the session would provide a different way in from the exercise suggested above. A good way to use them is to spread the pictures round the room, ask everyone to choose an image that appeals to them and say a little bit about their reason for choosing the picture.

Summary and example timings

Again, these are just a guide. The timings here allow for one brief buzz break during the teaching input.

	mins
Welcome	5
Opening exercise (How much do you know about Jesus?)	10
Jesus' birth	10
Jesus' ministry	10
Buzz groups	10
Jesus and the forgiveness of sins	10
Testimony	10
Who do you say I am?	10
Question time	10
Final summary and prayer	5
Coffee	

The life and ministry of Jesus

Jesus is central to our understanding of the Christian faith. He shows us who God is. He shows us what God is like. If you want to get to know the Christian faith – get to know Jesus.

Jesus is a historical figure. He really existed. The Gospels tell the story of his life and teaching. They were written within 50 years of his death. Each one is slightly different. Together they build a faithful portrait of who Jesus is.

Jesus' birth (Luke 1.26-38)

Christians believe that Jesus' birth and life and death are foretold in the prophets of the Old Testament. Jesus fulfils the hope of the Jewish people for an anointed king or Messiah who will bring salvation to God's people.

The message of Gabriel to Mary describes Jesus as the Son of God and a descendant of David, the great king of Israel who lived a thousand years before Jesus. The name Jesus means, in Hebrew, 'Saviour'. The word 'Christ' (the title given to Jesus) means, in Greek, 'anointed' and is the same word as the Hebrew 'Messiah'.

Jesus' ministry (Luke 4.16-24 and 38-44)

At the centre of Jesus' ministry is announcing the good news that he comes as God's anointed king to proclaim God's kingdom for the whole world.

Jesus proclaims the kingdom through his teaching in the synagogues and the temple and in the open air as crowds flock to him. As a sign that God's kingdom has come, Jesus heals the sick and drives out demons.

From the beginning of Jesus' ministry there are those who reject his message and even want to kill him.

Jesus and the forgiveness of sins (Luke 7.36-50)

Jesus proclaims a life-changing message for individuals who are far from God and rejected by society around them. This message is one of the forgiveness of sins (described here in the image of cancelling debts), a new beginning and acceptance by God and by the community of God's people. Again, Jesus proclaims this message not only by his words but also in his actions.

The woman responds to the message of forgiveness by deep devotion to Jesus but his actions provoke a different response among the Pharisees and a question from the crowd: 'Who is this who even forgives sins?'

Who do you say I am? (Luke 9.12-26)

In the miracle of the feeding of the five thousand, Jesus again demonstrates his care and compassion for people and the abundance of what God provides through him. Christians see in these miracles a foreshadowing of the service of Holy Communion as Jesus sustains his people in their journey.

The whole of the first part of the Gospel finds its focus in Jesus' question to Peter: 'Who do you say I am?' Jesus' words and actions have convinced us that this is no ordinary person. The people of Jesus' day and down the ages have their own theories. In the end, each disciple needs to hear Jesus' question and answer for ourselves.

> I see no escape from the dilemma: either Jesus is fraudulent, or his claim is true; either we judge him for being terribly amiss, or we let him judge us.
>
> Arthur Michael Ramsey,
> *Introducing the Christian Faith*, p. 41

As soon as the disciples recognize who Jesus is, the focus of the Gospel turns to Jesus' suffering and death and the meaning of his death for the world. Jesus also begins to explore with his followers the cost of discipleship.

For reflection

Spend time this week thanking God for the gift of his Son, Jesus Christ.

Continue your reading of the Gospel of Luke, looking back again at this week's passages.

The death and resurrection of Jesus

Introduction

Each of the four Gospels gives a huge amount of space to telling the story of the death and resurrection of Jesus. The Church has called this part of the Gospels the 'Passion Narrative' because it is the story of the love and the suffering of God in Christ. In Luke's Gospel Jesus begins to look ahead to the cross in chapter 9 – less than halfway through the book. There are some references in earlier chapters but in chapter 9 we have the first prediction of Jesus' death and, in verse 51, Jesus sets his face towards Jerusalem. The Passion story itself begins in chapter 22.

The aim of this session of the nurture course is to take time in telling of the death and resurrection of Jesus: to think about what happened and to begin to think about what it means. The structure of the session follows this pattern:

- *The story of the cross (video, reading or retelling).*

- *The meaning of the death of Jesus (input and questions).*

- *The story of the resurrection (reading or retelling).*

- *Evidence for the resurrection today (group exercise).*

- *The meaning of the resurrection (input and questions).*

- *Testimony.*

We have suggested placing the testimony at the end of the session this week in order to draw the different threads together. You will want to find a member of the group or the wider congregation who is able to weave honestly into their testimony some reflection on the death and resurrection of Jesus.

Introduction and welcome

Draw the group together at the beginning of the meeting in the normal way, remind the group of the material you covered in the last session and look ahead to this week's theme. There may be some questions outstanding from the last session. The account of the cross and resurrection only begins to make sense if people have at least some idea of who Jesus is: his character, his calling, his love for others and his teaching.

A helpful introduction can sometimes be to talk about the cross as a symbol of Christianity.

The story of the cross

Tell the story of the death of Jesus. There are different ways to do this. The simplest is to summarize and describe what happened in your own words, referring along the way to key parts of Luke's account, which the group is able to follow.

As an alternative, you could watch an extract from the *Jesus* video or the very moving crucifixion scene from Zeferelli's *Jesus of Nazareth*. Both extracts can be very powerful when watched in silence by a group.

For some (very literate) groups it may be helpful to read the final part of the Passion story together as a dramatized reading. You will find the text set out for this kind of reading in *Lent, Holy Week and Easter*. The Luke narrative is on pages 163–8.

The narrative of the death of Jesus is a very powerful story and has always formed a key element in Christian preaching and teaching. The traditional pattern of Holy Week enables all Christians to live in this story year by year. A key element in this session is simply to allow the Gospel message to speak to the group in a variety of ways.

However you tell the story, allow some time afterwards for people to respond. Keep a moment of quiet and then invite response as a whole group or suggest people talk to one another in twos and threes and put their response into words.

The meaning of the cross

Jesus says to the two disciples on the Emmaus road: 'Was it not necessary that the Messiah should suffer these things and then enter into his glory?'

In and through the death of Jesus the evil and chaos in creation are defeated and forgiveness and new life are offered to men and women everywhere.

The Bible and the Christian tradition have developed different ways of understanding this mystery of salvation. Some of these ways are explored on the members' handout. You may want to refer to them now and unpack the images behind them (the metaphor of friendship; the imagery of the legal system, of sacrifice or the marketplace). However, be careful not to be over technical. We will never understand completely *how* Jesus' death on the cross accomplishes this great victory over sin and death. At the heart of the Christian faith is not understanding things with our mind but placing our trust in what God has done for us in Christ.

Buzz groups and questions

Members of the group will need time to think about what they have heard. A time for buzz groups and questions should follow this section. The following questions may be helpful:

- *Which of these great pictures speaks to you about the meaning of Jesus' death?*

- *What questions do you have?*

The story of the resurrection

Tell the story of the resurrection, either through a simple Bible reading, or through telling the story in your own words. It may be helpful to give a brief survey of the different Gospel accounts of the resurrection. Each one has its own emphases.

The evidence for the resurrection

Invite the group to divide into buzz groups and invite each group to answer the question: How can we know that Jesus rose from the dead?

In most cases, the groups will be able to work out at least some of the evidence for themselves. Draw the groups back together and draw out from them the reasons they give. Summarize the findings on a large piece of paper. It is sometimes helpful if one of the group leaders role-plays a sceptic and asks hard questions of this evidence.

End this session by referring to the summary on the handout.

The meaning of the resurrection

Use the notes for Session 3 as a skeleton for a final input for the evening, summing up Sessions 2 and 3 of the course. It need not be too long and you do not need to refer to every point. Your main focus is the consequence and meaning of the resurrection at the heart of the Christian faith.

Testimony and conclusion

As mentioned above, a testimony is an excellent way to end the session, providing it links with the theme. As an alternative, you may want to read aloud this classical description of Christian coming to the cross, from John Bunyan's classic allegory, *The Pilgrim's Progress*. If this language is too complicated there are good illustrated children's versions.

Now I saw in my dream that the highway up which Christian was to go, was fenced on either side with a wall, and that wall was Salvation. Up this way, therefore, did burdened Christian run, but not without great difficulty, because of the load on his back. He ran thus till he came to a place somewhat ascending; and upon that place stood a Cross, and a little below, in the bottom, a Sepulchre. So I saw in my dream, that just as Christian came up with the Cross, his burden loosed from off his shoulders, and fell from off his back, and began to tumble, and so continued to do, till it came to the mouth of the Sepulchre, where it fell in, and I saw it no more. Then was Christian glad and lightsome, and said, with a merry heart, He hath given me rest by His sorrow, and life by His death. Then he stood awhile to look and wonder, for it was very surprising to him that the sight of the Cross should thus ease him of his burden. He looked, therefore, and looked again, even till springs that were in his head sent the waters down his cheeks. Now, as he stood looking and weeping, behold, three Shining Ones came to him and saluted him with 'Peace be to thee.' So the first said to him, 'Thy sins be forgiven thee'; the second stripped him of his rags, and clothed him with change of raiment; the third also set a mark on his forehead, and gave him a roll with a seal upon it, which he bade him look on as he ran, and that he should give it in at the Celestial Gate; so they went their way. Then Christian gave three leaps for joy and went out singing....

John Bunyan, *The Pilgrim's Progress*, pp. 52–3

To end the evening, you may want to read aloud or play a recording of a Christian hymn on the theme of the cross and resurrection such as 'When I survey' by Isaac Watts.

Reading for leaders

Read through the story of the cross and resurrection in the Gospel of Luke.

You will find more material on Jesus for this session in *Emmaus Growth Book 1: Knowing God* in the course 'Knowing Jesus'.

Chapter 5 of *The Mystery of Salvation*, 'Retelling the Story' may be a helpful guide to some of the ideas in this session. John Stott's excellent and clear study, *The Cross of Christ*, provides a very clear guide to images of the atonement, especially chapter 7, 'The Salvation of Sinners'. Michael Green's book, *The Day Death Died*, is clear, lively and helpful.

The first of the *Emmaus* Bible Resources, *The Lord is Risen!*, is a study of Luke's telling of the account of the resurrection in Luke 24.

Video and multimedia material

As for the Session 3.

Summary and example timings

	mins
Introduction and welcome	5
The story of the cross	15
The meaning of the cross	10
Buzz groups and questions	10
The story of the resurrection (reading or retelling)	5
The evidence for the resurrection (group exercise)	15
Buzz groups and questions	10
The meaning of the resurrection	10
Testimony	5
Final summary and prayer	5
Coffee	

The death and resurrection of Jesus

> Was it not necessary that the Messiah should suffer these things
> and then enter into his glory?
>
> Luke 24.26

Jesus tells his disciples that his death and resurrection are at the heart of his ministry.

The meaning of the cross

God made the world and loves the world, yet the world is full of chaos and suffering.

God calls us to a close relationship with him. But we have turned away from God. Our hearts are restless. We are cut off by the walls of pride and guilt and fear of change. We deserve to die.

God sent Jesus to save us from our sins and their effects (the name Jesus means 'Saviour'). Jesus died in our place so that we can enjoy a new relationship with God.

The Bible speaks of the meaning of Jesus' death in the great images of salvation.

■ *On the cross Jesus identified with our human predicament and took our place.*

■ *As a friend betrayed, Jesus deals with all that destroys relationships and offers restoration.*

■ *In his death, Jesus makes a new covenant between God and his people.*

■ *In his death, Jesus pays the penalty for sin.*

■ *Jesus is the Lamb of God who takes away the sin of the world.*

■ *In the cross, Jesus triumphs over all the powers of sin and evil.*

■ *In the cross, Jesus identifies with all the pain and suffering in the world.*

■ *On the cross, Jesus sets an example of perfect love.*

The evidence for the resurrection

The empty tomb

Jesus' tomb was empty on Easter Day, despite the guard on the grave.

If Jesus did not rise from the dead, where did his body go?

If the authorities had taken it (and why should they?) they would have produced it when claims about the resurrection were made later. The disciples were as surprised as anyone by the resurrection. Most of them were killed because of their faith in the resurrection of Jesus. It is impossible to believe that they took the body and told lies.

The witnesses

More than 500 people claimed to see Jesus alive.

Their encounter with the risen Jesus changed their lives and they were prepared to die for their belief.

The witnesses not only saw him, they talked with him, walked with him, learned from him, ate with him and touched him.

The Church began

After the cross, the disciples were demoralized and defeated. They were afraid of the Jews and denied that they had ever known Jesus.

Only a few days later they were risking their lives to proclaim Jesus as the Messiah. Their witness was to turn the world upside down. What event (other than the resurrection) could have so transformed the disciples?

The testimony of Christians

For nearly 2,000 years, in every culture, men and women have claimed that we can know the risen Christ for ourselves, today. (1 Corinthians 15.3-6)

The meaning of the resurrection

The resurrection gives us a completely new view of Jesus, of death and of life.

Jesus

- *Jesus really is God's Son.*

- *Jesus was crucified for our sins and rose again.*

- *Jesus is alive today.*

- *We can know him for ourselves.*

Death

- *Death is no longer something to be afraid of. Death has been conquered.*

- *Jesus has gone before to prepare a place for us (John 14.3).*

- *We shall all be raised to life with Christ.*

Life

- *Eternal life begins now, not when we die.*

- *Jesus gave his life for us. We give our lives back to him in love and service.*

- *Like the disciples, we are called to be witnesses to the power of the resurrection.*

For reflection

Reflect this week on the meaning of the cross and the resurrection.

Continue the Bible reading through Luke's Gospel.

The Holy Spirit

Introduction

From the teaching and discussion around the theme of God, our need of God and the ministry, death and resurrection of Jesus, the course now moves on to look at the ascension of Jesus, the Holy Spirit and the Spirit's work in our lives. Again, this is a large subject to tackle in a single session. This outline aims to lay a foundation of teaching and understanding, which can be built upon in the growth section of *Emmaus*, particularly through the course 'Come, Holy Spirit' (in *Growth Book 1*).

In the last 40 years there has been a great deal of fresh experience of the Holy Spirit's work and fresh thinking about the Spirit's role in the Christian life within many churches involved in charismatic renewal. The teaching content of this session builds on much of this thinking and experience. We have included an optional handout based on a question and answer session, which may be helpful in many churches where these issues are significant.

This session uses a wider range of biblical texts than are found in Luke's Gospel. You may want to use a set of Bibles with page numbers for this. Alternatively the main texts could be copied onto an extra handout.

Welcome and testimony

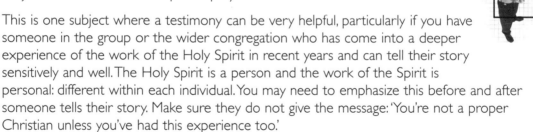

Welcome the group; look back briefly over the last four sessions; introduce the subject for this session and open in prayer.

This is one subject where a testimony can be very helpful, particularly if you have someone in the group or the wider congregation who has come into a deeper experience of the work of the Holy Spirit in recent years and can tell their story sensitively and well. The Holy Spirit is a person and the work of the Spirit is personal: different within each individual. You may need to emphasize this before and after someone tells their story. Make sure they do not give the message: 'You're not a proper Christian unless you've had this experience too.'

The Holy Spirit and you

Invite the group to break into small groups and ask people to share their own understanding and experience of the Holy Spirit. It may be helpful to refer briefly to the disciples Paul found in Ephesus. Some of the group may want to say: 'We have not even heard that there is a Holy Spirit' (Acts 19.2).

The following questions are suggested for the buzz groups:

Share together your own understanding and experience of the Holy Spirit in the Christian life.

- *Who is the Holy Spirit?*

- *Have you experienced the Spirit's work in your own life?*

■   *Have you any experience of the gifts of the Holy Spirit working in your life or in the lives of those you know?*

It is helpful to remember that the three great images of the Holy Spirit in the Bible can occur in the most gentle or dramatic forms and to reassure the group of this. The wind of the Spirit can be a gentle breath on the forehead of the disciples or the sound of a mighty wind. The fire of the Spirit can be a spark or a tongue of flame or a raging inferno. The rain of the Spirit can be a gentle dew, refreshing and renewing, or a great and drenching downpour. God deals with each of us at different times of our lives in different ways.

The term 'baptism in the Spirit' is a New Testament term, and we should not be afraid of using it today. The word 'baptism' in the New Testament is not so much a religious word as a very ordinary word for 'drenching'. If you walked under a window as someone was emptying a bucket of water, you would look up and say: 'Oi – you just baptized me, mate!' It is therefore a very appropriate expression for a time when someone has been drenched by the Holy Spirit – but a very unhelpful one if used to describe a particular experience every Christian has to pass through at a fixed stage on their journey.

The promise of the Holy Spirit

Draw the buzz groups together with a short plenary discussion and then go into the teaching content in this section, which sets the Holy Spirit in the context of the whole story of salvation.

Take particular care to explain that the Holy Spirit is a person of the Trinity, not an impersonal force or power. Even people who have been Christians for many years often refer to the Spirit as 'it'.

Tell the story of the work of the Holy Spirit in the Old Testament, using the notes on the handout as a guide. It is worthwhile pausing to note the story of the baptism of Jesus and then moving to the beginning of Acts. Tell the story of the ascension of Jesus and be clear that we live in the times between Christ's ascension and his return as king. The gift of the Spirit is for these times.

Tell the story of the day of Pentecost in your own words or read the Acts 2 narrative to the group. Give a brief description of Peter's sermon, ending by reading Acts 2.37-42.

The work of the Spirit

Stop for questions and a bit of discussion after the previous section and then go into the input on what the Holy Spirit does in our lives. Ideally, this should not be a monologue but interactive teaching. There are several biblical passages to read aloud in this section (not all from Luke's Gospel). You may like to allocate these among the more confident readers beforehand.

There are also several places where you can stop and ask people to do a little bit of thinking and reading on their own or in twos and threes. It is important to go at the pace of the group.

Buzz groups

At the end of the teaching session give people plenty of time to digest what has been said in small groups and to draw out a list of questions about the person and work of the Holy Spirit. The following questions will be helpful:

- *Have you experienced the Holy Spirit at work in your life?*

- *Have you experience of any of the spiritual gifts?*

- *What questions do you still have?*

Question time and plenary

There will probably be no shortage of questions this week, particularly about the work of the Holy Spirit in our lives and the gifts of the Spirit.

Talking about some of the gifts of the Spirit, such as tongues, prophecy and healing, can be fascinating and attractive to some enquirers but really off-putting to others. It is important to learn how to talk about the gifts of the Spirit and answer questions about them in a normal and natural way that allows some people to go on and go deeper in this area at the present time and others to be able to say: 'I think I'll just leave this one for now.'

Some questions and answers

You may answer all of these questions as part of the plenary. If so, all well and good. However, if you do not, it is worth running through them quickly at the end of the session and giving out the supplementary handout to correct some common misunderstandings about the work of the Holy Spirit. End, if you can, by reading together Luke 11.9-13.

Looking ahead

Close the session by giving a preview of next week's meeting, which will be on the subject of 'Becoming a Christian'. Emphasize that next week will pull together the whole of the first part of the course and that it is very important not to miss the session. There will be a chance to meet and talk with individuals after Session 6 but it is worth giving a preliminary invitation after this meeting in case anyone wants to talk further about the work of the Holy Spirit. End the session with a period of quiet prayer based around the prayer or the song 'Spirit of the living God' or one of the traditional hymns to the Holy Spirit such as 'Come down O love divine' or 'Come, Holy Ghost, our souls inspire' (to be found, for example, in *Mission Praise*).

Reading for leaders

Read and prepare the Bible passages thoroughly with the help of a simple commentary.

You will find more material for this session in *Emmaus Growth Book 1: Knowing God* in the course 'Come, Holy Spirit'. See pages 114–115 for a discussion of the two passages from John's Gospel; pages 124–5 for a discussion of Galatians 5 and pages 134–5 for a discussion of gifts of the Spirit.

For more on the doctrine of the Holy Spirit see Michael Green, *I Believe in the Holy Spirit*. For more on each of the gifts of the Spirit see David Pytches, *Come, Holy Spirit*.

Summary and example timings

	mins
Welcome	5
Testimony	10
The Holy Spirit and you	15
The promise of the Holy Spirit	15
The work of the Spirit	20
Buzz groups and question time	20
Final summary and prayer	5
Coffee	

The Holy Spirit

> Then afterwards, I will pour out my spirit on all flesh;
> your sons and your daughters shall prophesy, your old men will dream dreams,
> and your young men will see visions.
> Even on the male and female slaves, in those days, I will pour out my spirit.
>
> Joel 2. 28-29

The promise of the Holy Spirit

In Old Testament days the Holy Spirit was not given to every believer. The Spirit of God rested on great national leaders (like Moses); great prophets (like Elijah); great kings (like David) and on other special individuals.

The coming of the Holy Spirit on these people was a definite event that made a real difference to their lives.

But the prophets foretold a time when God would pour out his Holy Spirit upon all people.

The Holy Spirit came down upon Jesus at his baptism in the Jordan (Luke 3.22).

According to Luke, after Jesus rose from the dead, he met with the disciples over 40 days before he was taken into heaven – the event the Church calls the Ascension. Jesus promised that, after his ascension, the Holy Spirit would be given to his disciples.

This is what happened on the day of Pentecost. The disciples' lives were completely transformed.

The same promise of the Holy Spirit is given to every Christian today.

> Jesus ordered them not to leave Jerusalem, but to wait there for the promise of the Father. 'This', he said, 'is what you have heard from me; for John baptized with water; but you will be baptized with the Holy Spirit not many days from now.'
>
> Acts 1. 4-5

The work of the Spirit

The Spirit dwells within us

The Holy Spirit fills that space in our lives that no one else can fill. The Spirit comforts, teaches, counsels and guides us and reveals Jesus to us.

Look at these passages from John's Gospel together. In small groups, make a summary of what the passages teach us about the Holy Spirit's work:

John 14.15-27

John 16.5-16.

Emmaus Nurture course handout: The Holy Spirit

The Spirit makes us more like Jesus

When you become a Christian you don't become perfect. There's still a lot to put right in your action and character.

The Holy Spirit works within us, transforming us so that we reflect more and more the character of Jesus.

He brings out in our lives the fruits of the Holy Spirit.

Look them up in Galatians 5.22-23 and make a list together.

The Spirit gives us gifts and empowers us for ministry

Jesus invites us to proclaim the gospel. But we can't do that on our own. The Holy Spirit empowers us to share in this work.

As an important part of that empowering we are given spiritual gifts. Some gifts mean that we have God's anointing in a special way on our natural gifts (in such things as hospitality, teaching, administration or evangelism).

Others are supernatural gifts such as praying in tongues (a special prayer language God gives), prophecy (speaking God's word into different situations) or healing.

Gifts are given to every Christian who desires them and seeks to build up the life and mission of the Church.

Lists of gifts of the Spirit are given in 1 Corinthians 12.1-11 and Romans 12.6-8. Look at the passages in small groups and make a list of the gifts here. Put an asterisk by any you don't understand. The greatest gift of all is love (1 Corinthians 13).

For reflection

Spend time this week thanking God for the gift of the Spirit. You may want to make the prayer your own: Spirit of the living God, fall afresh on me.

Continue your reading of the Gospel of Luke. Aim to finish the Gospel this week if you can.

The Holy Spirit:
Some questions and answers

Is the Holy Spirit at work in every Christian?

Yes, the Spirit is at work in every Christian. Paul writes that no one can say 'Jesus is Lord' except by the Holy Spirit (1 Corinthians 12.3). Even before you became a Christian, God was at work in your life in many ways – and that work continues now.

Is there a definite experience of baptism (or drenching) in the Holy Spirit?

Yes, there is. The Bible speaks of this experience and it is part of the Christian life today. Jesus experienced such an anointing by the Holy Spirit at his baptism (Luke 3.22) even though the Holy Spirit was active in his life before. The disciples experienced the work and power of the Spirit before Pentecost, but they still needed the empowering at Pentecost before their new ministry could begin.

When should I expect it to happen?

At the time that is right for you. We can't put the Holy Spirit in a box. God is in charge. For some people there is a definite experience of the Holy Spirit at conversion, or near to that point. For other people there is a definite experience of the Holy Spirit's empowering months, or years, later. For others both conversion and being filled with the Spirit happen gradually and slowly over a long period of time.

The experience you have of God's power at work in your life now is more important than the way you received it.

Is this a once and for all event?

No. There's much more to come. Paul tells the Ephesian Christians to go on being filled with the Spirit (Ephesians 5.18). The disciples are filled with the Spirit over and over again in Acts. The process of being renewed by the Holy Spirit goes on until we are with the Lord.

How do we receive the gift of the Holy Spirit?

We simply ask (Luke 11.9-13).

How do I know I have received the Holy Spirit?

If we are people in whom the Spirit has been moving gradually in our lives over the years, we may not always know whether we have received the Holy Spirit. We do not necessarily feel any different. Paul tells us that the work of the Holy Spirit can be told by the fruit that is produced. This is the best test. If your life in Christ is bearing fruit then you have received the Holy Spirit.

Becoming a Christian

Introduction

The goal of this session is to draw together all that has gone before. For the first five sessions you will have been addressing the group as if they were all interested enquirers (even though some of them may have been Christians for many years). You have covered the basics of what Christians believe about God the Father and creator, about our need of God, about Jesus and the Holy Spirit. This session pulls this teaching together into a very simple outline of the gospel based upon the Apostles' Creed, puts the challenge of Christian commitment to each member of the group and focuses on our private and public response to God's grace.

Key decisions

There are three key decisions to take in respect of this session, which need to be thought through in terms of your general church policy with the Nurture course, and adjusted in the light of each group's journey.

The first decision is *where to place this session in the course*. We have retained it at this point in the outline of the material, drawing together the thinking in Part 1 of the nurture course. There is a certain logic in looking together at what a Christian is before thinking about how Christians grow. However, experience suggests that, for some groups, this may be too early in the journey. It may be more helpful to have the session after Part 2 (which is where we have placed the equivalent session in *Youth Emmaus*).

The second decision is *how to build a link between this session in the life of the group and public worship*. Some members of the group will be preparing for baptism and/or confirmation at the end of the course. Others will find it appropriate to make an affirmation of baptismal faith in the context of public worship, perhaps during a service of baptism and confirmation. However, others in the group may as yet be undecided about the Christian faith. Many churches will find it helpful, therefore, to offer a Service of Welcome at this point to those in the group who wish to make use of it and announce their intention to be baptized, confirmed or make an affirmation of baptismal faith. An order of service for this purpose can be found on pages 108–109.

The third question is *how to support individual members of the group in their journey of faith*. Ideally, this session needs to be followed by some time spent by the leaders or co-leaders with each member of the group, talking through how they are getting on with the course so far; discussing particular questions that have not yet been answered in the main sessions; helping each person to discern where they may be in their journey and, if it seems appropriate, praying together in the way that is right for that person. Some guidelines for these individual interviews are given in the following section (see pages 43–4). You need to agree a policy on them as a group of leaders (how will they be offered, what timescale you will work on?) before you offer this session.

Words for prayer

In the material for this session we have offered words for prayer, which can be used in one of three ways:

- *Individually by members of the group.*
  Some word of explanation is given at the session. Individuals use the order of prayer on their own and, if they wish, talk this through with the leaders of the nurture group.

- *As a form of prayer for use by one or two members of the group with the leaders.*
  If it seems appropriate, as part of the individual interview, the leaders offer to pray with the group member(s) either at that time or in a separate appointment, adapting the order of prayer to individual circumstances.

- *As a form of service involving the whole group with opportunity for prayer and laying on of hands.*

The group takes a separate session to meet for worship and prayer and make a response together to the grace of God through the words provided. The service includes the opportunity to receive prayer with the laying on of hands.

Two examples

The leaders of *Group A* make a provisional plan for this session at the beginning of the course and meet after Session 4 to review progress in the group. Their discernment is that trust is developing well in the group and it is right to offer the session on 'Becoming a Christian' in Week 6. They agree to offer to meet with group members individually and pray with them as appropriate in the three weeks or so after Week 5. They arrange with the vicar to incorporate a simple Service of Welcome into the Sunday Eucharist after Week 8. A service of baptism and confirmation (including Affirmation of Baptismal Faith) is to be held two weeks after the nurture group ends.

The leaders of *Group B* also meet after Session 4. Their discernment is that the group is at a much earlier stage. Attendance has been inconsistent, therefore community is growing only slowly. Several members of the group are still clearly very much at the stage of being enquirers with lots of questions. They decide to offer this session as Week 6 but in a very low-key way, with individual interviews offered over the second part of the course and no Service of Welcome on a Sunday morning at this stage. However, the leaders decide to offer an additional session for the group and their sponsors after Week 10 as a Service of Affirmation of Faith with opportunity for prayer and laying on of hands. The candidates are still invited to join in a service of Baptism, Confirmation and Affirmation of Faith that takes place in a neighbouring parish towards the end of the course. This is followed by a short Service of Welcome in the candidates' own church on the following Sunday.

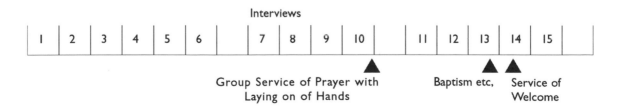

As Session 6 is one of the most important of the whole course, it is also wise to be very diligent in prayer for the members of the group during the week beforehand and for the session itself. You may want to enlist the help of other individuals or groups in the church here. It is surprising how situations have arisen to prevent people being present for this particular meeting.

Welcome and testimony

Welcome the group as previously: open in prayer and introduce the theme for the session. A testimony can be helpful – but it is not a good idea to bring a stranger into the group. You want the discussion to be as open as possible. If possible, the testimony should focus on the process of Christian commitment and also the cost of discipleship.

Sharing your story

By now people should be fairly familiar with the idea of a journey to faith. It may be worth reminding them of the lost son exercise in Session 2. Ask them to focus on the following questions in small groups of three or four. If you use the middle question you will need to print out a copy or write the questions on a large piece of paper.

Share your story of your journey to faith. Are you a Christian? How did you come to faith?

Can you say what is incomplete about these descriptions of what a Christian is?

- *I went to Sunday School.*

- *I'm as good as him.*

- *I believe in God.*

- *We were married in church.*

- *I enjoy Songs of Praise.*

- *I was baptized as a baby.*

- *I'm not anything else.*

- *My wife goes.*

How would you describe a Christian?

Unpack the discussion as a whole group. Run through the list of definitions of a Christian. Ask people to call out what is wrong with each one. Then ask each group to describe a Christian for you. It may help to write the different definitions down on a flip chart.

What is a Christian?

It should be fairly easy then to pick up from the plenary discussion and run through the teaching points in this section. Each is important and needs to be illustrated and expanded on so that the group grasps what is meant. If necessary, stop along the way for questions, comments and feedback.

The Christian gospel

The aim here is to pull together the teaching of the last five sessions. A change of voice may be useful.

The Christian faith is summarized on the supplementary handout in the words of the Apostles' Creed, one of four key Christian texts handed on to new Christians in the Nurture course. Almost all of the elements in the Apostles' Creed have been addressed in the first five sessions of the course. The two lines on the Church and the communion of saints will be explored a little more in the session on 'Belonging to the Church' in Part 2.

Look together at the summary of the Christian gospel, which follows the creed on the sheet. This section stresses the fourfold response of repentance, faith, membership of the Church (signified by baptism) and receiving the promised gift of the Spirit. This is the full Christian response, which is found all through the Acts of the Apostles when people are invited to become Christians.

Buzz groups and plenary

It is worth spending time in small groups digesting this simple presentation of the gospel and of the response we need to make to God's grace. Ask people to draw out anything they don't yet understand or are not sure about. Think these through together in plenary.

Baptism

Baptism is the great sacrament that marks people coming to faith and membership of the Church. It is important, therefore, to give clear teaching about baptism at this point in the Nurture course as part of the basics of Christian faith (Hebrews 6.1-2).

As a useful visual aid, it can be helpful to place a font or large bowl of water in the centre of the room for this part of the meeting. It will be important also to talk about baptism by immersion.

As you go through the different elements in a baptism service, it may be helpful to link the different parts with the fourfold response of repentance, faith, receiving the gift of the Spirit and membership of the Church. You may also want to explore the way in which these elements find their expression in the baptism service of your own church. You will need to address those who have been baptized as infants and may want to affirm their baptismal faith at this point in their lives and those who were baptized as infants but have not yet been confirmed.

Because the *Emmaus* Nurture course is intended to be used by a number of different Churches, we have not included any texts on this handout apart from the Apostles' Creed. The supplementary handout contains texts based on the Church of England *Common Worship: Initiation Services*.

Buzz groups

Again, follow this section on baptism with an opportunity for people to talk in small groups about whether they have been baptized and confirmed and to articulate any questions about baptism that may arise. Follow this time in buzz groups with a question time.

How do I become a Christian?

Emphasize the importance of making a clear commitment to Christ for those who are on a journey of coming to faith: the moment at which you pass from being an outsider looking in to someone who is on the inside of the Christian faith; when you change from being an enquirer to becoming a new Christian. For some this process of commitment may be very gradual; for others more sudden – but it is a step along the journey everyone needs to make.

You will need to explain at this point your offer of an individual conversation with members of the group and how to go about arranging that. You will also need to give notice of what you have decided to suggest in terms of special services for the group or the opportunity to make a response through public worship.

In the way you present this material you need to avoid anything that might pressurize people or make them think they need to make a decision or a response of faith either at that moment or in the next two weeks. Say clearly and explicitly that some in the group will have reached this point some time ago and others may be nowhere near it yet. Still others will want to make their baptism (or confirmation) that moment of clear decision and commitment. But everyone needs some understanding of Christian commitment and how it is made through prayer.

Explain that an act of commitment needs to be made publicly at some stage but that it is also helpful to make such an act either privately or in prayer with one or two others. The prayers in the supplementary handout are provided for that purpose. If you are using the sheet, talk briefly through each section and read the prayer aloud.

Ending the evening

There are a number of different possibilities. You will need some idea beforehand but be sensitive to the group and to the Holy Spirit.

■   *In prayer. It may be appropriate to lead the group through the act of commitment to Christ with each person having the opportunity to pray silently as the leader says the words.*

■   *With buzz groups, discussion and prayer. The groups could either digest this business of commitment further or look at the 'going forward' question in the members' handout.*

■   *With a short video, testimony or piece of music – as a further invitation to follow Christ.*

In all cases close the meeting in prayer and give a clear pointer forward to next week – the start of Part 2 of the course and a look at how Christians pray.

Coffee

It is particularly important this week to mix with the group and talk briefly, if possible, with each person before they leave.

Reading for leaders

Chapter 1 of *Travelling Well*, called 'Beginning the Way', is all about baptism and would be good preparatory reading. See also *Baptism* by Michael Green, the Commentary by the Church of England Liturgical Commission in *Initiation Services* pages 185ff. and other guides to *Common Worship* or the initiation services in your own Church.

Summary and example timings

	mins
Welcome	5
Testimony	5
Sharing your story	10
What is a Christian?	5
The Christian gospel	15
Buzz groups and plenary	10
Baptism	10
Buzz groups and question time	10
How do I become a Christian?	15
Final summary and prayer	5
Coffee	

Individual interviews after Session 6

It may be that some people will not want to have an individual session but most will probably be glad to talk things through on an individual basis. As a team of leaders you will need to plan who will meet with each person, involving sponsors in the process wherever possible. One-to-one meetings are probably best, provided the leader and group member are the same sex. If they are not, then someone else should normally be present.

The key to spending time with someone on their own is, of course, careful listening. Every person's experience and story will be different. Avoid coming to the meeting with any preconceptions at all about what should happen – other than that you are going to listen carefully and attentively. After some general conversation at the beginning simply invite the group member to tell you the story so far of their journey to faith. People will choose various starting points – but, almost certainly, these will be years before they ever came to the Nurture course.

The listening will take time. It probably won't be hard, but be as responsive a listener as you can. Where necessary keep the story on track, but otherwise don't interrupt. At the end of the person's story there are three questions it is good to have ready to ask (if this seems right):

1   Where do you think you are now in your relationship with God?

2   Have you any remaining questions?

3   Is there anything you would like us to pray through?

It may not be appropriate to ask all three questions with each person – and some may have been answered already through their story. If there are any remaining questions, talk these through as best you can.

At this point you will need to decide whether it is appropriate that you should pray together and how you should pray. Obviously great sensitivity is needed both to the person and to the Holy Spirit's leading and guiding. There are any number of paths you could follow. As you become experienced in this ministry you will be able to work out your own. In the meantime, here are some suggestions:

If the person has a great many questions still, no prayer at all or just a simple prayer for God's blessing on their search may be best. It may be that many of the questions and barriers will be overcome through the next part of *Emmaus* and that you will be able to go further in another individual session towards the end of the course.

The person may be ready to make an individual act of commitment, following the prayers in the supplementary handout. Talk this through with them and then lead them step by step through the stages of repentance, faith, a prayer to be filled with the Holy Spirit and a promise to serve and be part of God's Church. After the prayer to be filled with the Spirit, it may be appropriate (with the person's permission) to lay hands on the person's head and pray for them to be filled with the Spirit. When you pray with people in this way sometimes there will be very obvious signs that God is at work: a sense of his presence, tears, perhaps speaking in tongues or some other spiritual gift. Sometimes there will be no such 'obvious' signs. What is happening has to be received by faith. The sense of change and of the presence of Christ in the person's life will come gradually and steadily over the weeks to come.

Other pastoral conversations

You may want to talk through the possibility of the person making an individual confession at this point in their journey of faith. Many people come to Christ with a great many things on their conscience. Talk through with them what that would mean and how that would be arranged in your own church.

There may be some specific barriers to faith. The most common will be some area of bitterness where a person has been wronged and needs to forgive before they can move on to a full commitment. Others can be aspects of their present lifestyle; involvement in the occult, past or present; or pressure within the family.

The person may have been a Christian for many years but is ready now to make a renewed commitment of faith. The order of words in the Members' Handout is suitable for this.

For many new Christians this is the time to encourage them to build good habits and disciplines of Sunday worship. It is important to set high standards and expectations here and to explain as simply as possible that part of being a Christian is to be in church every Sunday: to give time to God first and build the rest of your week around that rather than fitting God into your spare time. If people simply resolve to come to church 'a bit more often' they are opening themselves to spiritual conflict and temptation each Sunday, as they have to decide each week whether or not they will come to worship. It is very easy to say: 'I'll miss today and go next week.' Once the decision has been made 'that on Sunday morning (or evening) I will be in church', then a lot of the battle about whether to come or not disappears.

The individual time with people is an excellent opportunity to discuss how the person feels about taking part in any Services of Welcome your church feels are appropriate to offer. These should already have been mentioned within the group sessions. Make it clear that people are welcome to continue as part of the group even if they do not feel able to take part with integrity in the public services.

Finally, when time has run out or you draw naturally to a conclusion, make a good ending to the session. Thank the person for their time. Encourage them in whatever way is appropriate and make your departure.

Becoming a Christian

What is a Christian?

■ *Many people in our society believe themselves to be Christians but have only begun to understand the Christian faith.*

■ *Being a Christian is not something vague and private but definite and public.*

■ *No one is born as a Christian (although you may be born into a Christian family). No one becomes a Christian by accident either.*

■ *You become a Christian by making a decision to say yes to God's gracious invitation to follow Jesus Christ.*

■ *The sign of a person responding to God's call in this way and becoming part of the Church is the sign of baptism.*

The Christian gospel

The Christian Church down the ages has summarized the Christian faith in the words of the Apostles' Creed.

At the heart of the gospel are these truths:

God made us and loves us.

We were made to know God but we have turned away from his love.

God sent his Son, Jesus, to draw the world back to him.

Jesus lived a life without sin.

He died on the cross. God raised him from the dead.

Through Jesus, God offers to everyone:

■ *forgiveness of sins;*

■ *a new relationship with God and with God's people;*

■ *the gift of eternal life;*

■ *the call to service and discipleship.*

God invites us to say yes — to respond to this gracious gift.

Our response is fourfold:

■ *repentance;*

■ *faith;*

- *receiving the promised gift of the Holy Spirit;*
- *becoming a full member of the Church.*

Baptism

Jesus was baptized in water by John at the River Jordan.

Following Jesus' command, from earliest times, baptism has been the outward sign of a Christian's response to the call of God to follow Christ.

In the service of baptism the candidates publicly turn away from all they know to be wrong and turn to Christ.

The candidates declare their faith in God, Father, Son and Holy Spirit.

Baptism in water is a sign of a new beginning as the water symbolizes being made clean. Going down into the waters of baptism is also a symbol of dying with Christ and rising again.

The congregation prays for the candidates to be given the gift of the Holy Spirit and they are welcomed into membership of the Church.

In our baptism we are commissioned to live as Christian disciples and to share in God's mission to the world.

How do I become a Christian?

Becoming a Christian is a journey that may take months, sometimes years.

Significant points in the journey are often marked by making an appropriate response through personal prayer, prayer with others or public worship.

Such moments of response might include:

- *baptism as a child or an adult;*
- *confirmation;*
- *making a personal commitment through prayer to follow Christ;*
- *prayer to receive the gift of the Holy Spirit;*
- *a public Affirmation of Baptismal Faith;*
- *prayer with others at a new period in your life and Christian service.*

For reflection

Spend time this week thinking about what all this means for you and perhaps using some of the prayers on the sheet.

Emmaus Nurture course handout: Becoming a Christian

Becoming a Christian:
Prayers in response to God's grace

These words and prayers are provided to guide you in your own prayers of response in the areas of repentance, faith, receiving the gift of the Spirit and responding to God's call to worship and mission as part of the Church. Each can be used on its own or in sequence. You can pray them yourself or with others.

Prayers of confession

Lord Jesus Christ, Son of God, have mercy on me a sinner.

This prayer is best said quietly and repeated as part of your preparation.

> Do you reject the devil and all rebellion against God?
> **I reject them.**
> Do you renounce the deceit and corruption of evil?
> **I renounce them.**
> Do you repent of the sins that separate us from God and neighbour?
> **I repent of them.**
> Do you turn to Christ as Saviour?
> **I turn to Christ.**
> Do you submit to Christ as Lord?
> **I submit to Christ.**
> Do you come to Christ, the way, the truth and the life?
> **I come to Christ.**

From the Baptism Service, p. 36 in *Common Worship: Initiation Services*

Declaration of faith

The Apostles' Creed can be said at this point.

> I believe in God, the Father almighty,
> creator of heaven and earth.
>
> I believe in Jesus Christ, his only Son, our Lord,
> who was conceived by the Holy Spirit,
> born of the Virgin Mary,
> suffered under Pontius Pilate,
> was crucified, died, and was buried;
> he descended to the dead.
> On the third day he rose again;
> he ascended into heaven,
> he is seated at the right hand of the Father,
> and he will come to judge the living and the dead.

I believe in the Holy Spirit,
the holy catholic Church,
the communion of saints,
the forgiveness of sins,
the resurrection of the body,
and the life everlasting. Amen.

I answer the call of God my creator.
I trust in Jesus Christ as my Saviour.
I seek new life from the Holy Spirit.

From *Common Worship: Initiation Services*, p. 168

Come, Holy Spirit

Come now, Lord Jesus Christ and dwell in my life
Fill me with your Holy Spirit
Strengthen me for your service
And empower me with your love.

Commitment to worship and mission

Those who are baptized are called to worship and serve God.

Will you continue in the apostles' teaching and fellowship, in the breaking of bread, and in the prayers?
With the help of God, I will.
Will you persevere in resisting evil, and, whenever you fall into sin, repent and return to the Lord?
With the help of God, I will.
Will you proclaim by word and example the good news of God in Christ?
With the help of God, I will.
Will you seek and serve Christ in all people, loving your neighbour as yourself?
With the help of God, I will.
Will you acknowledge Christ's authority over human society, by prayer for the world and its leaders, by defending the weak, and by seeking peace and justice?
With the help of God, I will.

From *Common Worship: Initiation Services*, p. 170

How Christians grow

Introduction

Part 1 of the *Emmaus* Nurture course looks at what Christians believe. Part 2 focuses on how Christians grow. The four sessions are loosely based on Acts 2.42, which describes how the first new Christians spent their time after the day of Pentecost. The emphasis is on equipping the members of the group to continue to grow as Christians for the whole of their lives.

Each of the four subjects of prayer, Bible reading, belonging to the Church and Holy Communion can form a course in itself (and indeed there is a four- or five-week module on each unit in the *Emmaus* growth material). However, it is important for new Christians to have at least a foundation laid in each area at the start of their Christian lives.

As with Part 1 of the course, there is still need for good-quality teaching input although there is a slightly richer diet of exercises and things to do. These focus more on the subject matter and less on people telling their story. In Part 1 everyone was addressed as an interested enquirer (even though some may have been Christians for many years). In Part 2, all should be addressed in the teaching sessions as though they are very new Christians (even though some have been in the faith for many years and others still haven't reached that point of commitment). It often happens that those who are still enquiring and asking questions are helped by the less directly evangelistic teaching in Part 2 of the course. Eyes are opened to just how much there is to Christianity and the Christian faith.

Travelling Well is an excellent handbook for this part of the course and has chapters that correspond to each of the sessions (Chapters 3 to 6) together with a selection of prayers and readings.

Learning to pray

Introduction

This session aims to give some simple teaching about prayer, to introduce the idea of daily personal prayer and, if there is time, to cover the basics of praying together as a group.

The parable of the sower is to this section of the course what the parable of the two sons is to Part 1. It is, therefore, important to cover the material even though it may not be directly relevant to prayer. The parable gives a basic framework for people to understand the process of Christian growth, changing the metaphor from the journey (of the younger son) to the growth of the seed.

Another dimension of the group's life to begin to develop in different ways from this point is worship and prayer together. The way you do this will depend very much on the tradition, style and spirituality of your own church and the resources you have available. The leaders' guide suggests a number of ways to develop this over the coming weeks but feel free, as ever, to adapt this to what is appropriate in your own situation. You may want to introduce singing together or shared prayer or to use a simple liturgical form of prayer. As a way of marking the time of prayer and worship, the group may find it helpful to have a visual focus, such as lighting a candle. In many groups, trust will now have grown to the point where people are able to mention particular requests for prayer and, over time, to begin to pray for one another. This session makes an important beginning in exploring with the group the words of the Lord's Prayer.

In building up the life of the Nurture group from this point, bear in mind what you hope may happen at the end of the course, particularly if the group is to continue to meet as a small Christian community and with its own life and ministry.

Testimony is not included in the next four sessions partly for reasons of space, and partly so that the membership of the group can be as stable as possible during this important middle period of its life.

Welcome and introduction

A short welcome and look back at the last session. Open in prayer and give a brief preview of the next four sessions and outline why they are important, referring to Acts 2.42. Explain any differences in style and approach for this second part of the course.

The parable of the sower

Ask a member of the group, who has prepared the passage beforehand, to read the parable from Luke's Gospel and then ask the group to talk in small groups. The groups should share together anything significant about their Christian life following the last session and reflect together on the different kinds of soil and what they mean. One possible exercise is to invite the groups to invent a story or think of someone who illustrates one of the soil types.

As the groups come back together, draw out some of the key lessons from the parable:

- *The seed on the path: reflect on the times in the past when members of the group may have heard the Christian message but it has made no difference to their lives.*

- *The seed on the rock: remind the group that not every seed that takes root bears fruit. There can often be an important time of grace and joy at the beginning of someone's Christian life. We need to be aware that times of testing come for every Christian in different ways and that we need to persevere in these times.*

- *The seed among thorns: the difficulties that beset these young plants come mainly from good things in life, which can be a distraction from following Christ. What are the 'cares, riches and pleasures of life'?*

- *The seed on good soil: seed in good soil takes time to grow to maturity. So do new Christians. Most of us need particular teaching, encouragement and support during that time. The fruit can mean both our character (the fruits of the Spirit) and good things that happen because of our influence and Christian service.*

Have a few minutes for any questions arising from the parable.

Buzz groups

Introduce the main subject for this evening, learning to pray, and invite people to talk together in small groups about their experience of prayer. Make sure you give permission for people to articulate a range of different experiences. Depending on the group, you may or may not want to gather together the different experiences in the whole group.

Lord, teach us to pray

This section introduces the Lord's Prayer. Guide the group through each part of the prayer, taking care to explain any terms that may be unfamiliar. You may want to give the group as a supplementary handout the sheet 'Praying the Lord's Prayer' (*Growth Book 2: Growing as a Christian*, p. 33) which sets out a simple framework for praying the Lord's Prayer.

The next two Bible passages aim to establish that it is good for Christians to pray both on their own and together.

Buzz groups and questions

Invite the group to talk together about the different reasons why it is healthy and important for Christians to develop good habits of prayer – and what some of the difficulties might be.

As you draw out from the group what they have shared, it may help to mention:

- *Prayer builds our friendship with God. Like any relationship, our relationship with God will develop and grow as we spend quality time on building the friendship.*

- *Prayer was a vital part of Jesus' own ministry (Mark 1.35). How can we neglect it?*

- *We grow more like the Lord as we spend more time with him.*

- *Prayer strengthens us for our daily lives.*

- *Through prayer God's power is released in the world, in the Church and in our own lives.*

Some first steps

Give a brief introduction to different ways of planning and building prayer time. Mention Bible reading notes (it may help to have some samples this week and next). Undated notes are generally best for very new Christians.

Refer to the possibility of using a simple outline for prayer such as a Daily Office. Again you may want to have some samples there. *Common Worship: Daily Prayer* might be offered, together with any helps for prayer you have developed in your own church.

If there is a lot of interest in prayer through a Daily Office, build some time into the next session to explore that in more depth and detail. If the leaders do not feel qualified to lead such a session, consider inviting in someone who can.

Whichever form for daily prayer is used there will still be elements of preparing, listening and talking. Introduce these briefly and then ask people to complete the exercise in the Members' Handout in small groups.

Question time and plenary

In small groups discuss together the importance of each part in your prayer time. Give as many ways as you can think of for preparing to pray, listening to God and talking to him.

Draw together the group's suggestions for preparing, listening and talking on a flip chart or overhead projector slide. If there are any obvious omissions you may like to put them in yourself. Move then into a general question and answer session on prayer and how to pray.

Praying with others

It is important that this is dealt with properly and not rushed so, if you are by now a little pressed for time, delay it and make time at the beginning of the next session.

Explain why prayer in small groups is important. Also explain that it can be difficult – especially at first. Go through the suggestions for how to pray in the members' handout. You may want to think together about how the group members themselves would find it helpful to support one another in prayer.

Prayer and worship

Try to develop a way of praying together that will become a pattern over the weeks to come. In the intercessions section, at an appropriate point in the group's life, allow some space for people to pray aloud (but when you give the invitation make it clear that the group can continue to pray in silence).

A possible order for Evening Prayer for nurture groups in included in the liturgical material at the end of the book.

End by saying the Lord's Prayer together.

Coffee

You may want to have a small bookstall or lending library available with different books and helps in prayer.

Reading for leaders

There are good resources available on learning to pray. The *Emmaus* growth course on 'Learning to Pray' (in *Growth Book 2: Growing as a Christian*) is based around the Lord's Prayer.

Travelling Well, chapter three, 'Learning to Pray'.

Stephen Cottrell, *Praying Through Life.*

Robert Warren, *An Affair of the Heart.*

John Pritchard, *Learning to Pray.*

Michael Ramsey, *Be Still and Know.*

Resources for group members

You may want to make copies of all the above available for group members to look and borrow together with copies of *Common Worship: Daily Prayer* or material your own church has developed and some Bible reading notes. The *Emmaus* Bible Resources also contain a simple order for Daily Prayer to be used together with the Bible reading notes.

Summary and example timings

	mins
Welcome and introduction	5
The parable of the sower (groups and plenary)	15
Buzz groups on experience of prayer	10
Lord, teach us to pray	15
Buzz groups and questions	10
Some first steps	10
Question time	5
Praying with others	10
Prayer and worship	10
Coffee	

Learning to pray

In this part of *Emmaus* we will be thinking together about how Christians grow: through prayer, reading the Bible, fellowship and worship (especially through Holy Communion).

> They devoted themselves to the apostles' teaching and fellowship, to the breaking of bread and the prayers. Acts 2.42

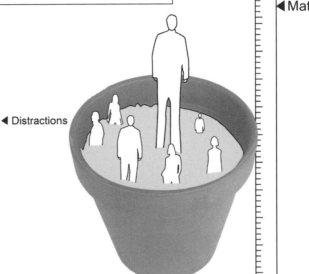

◀ Maturity

◀ Distractions

The parable of the sower

Luke 8.1-15.

Jesus tells this story to teach us lessons about how Christians grow to maturity and what dangers and distractions to expect.

■   *The seed on the path*

■   *The seed on the rock*

■   *The seed among thorns*

■   *The seed on good soil.*

Lord, teach us to pray (Luke 11.1)

Jesus responds to the disciples' question by giving them his own prayer which is the foundation of every Christian's life of prayer.

Our Father in heaven,
hallowed be your name,
your kingdom come,
your will be done,
on earth as in heaven.
Give us today our daily bread.
Forgive us our sins
as we forgive those who sin against us.
Lead us not into temptation
but deliver us from evil.
For the kingdom, the power,
and the glory are yours
now and for ever. Amen.

Jesus encourages the disciples to develop good habits of personal prayer…

> Whenever you pray, go into your room and shut the door and pray to your Father who is in secret; and your Father who sees in secret will reward you.   Matthew 6.6

… and of prayer together:

> Where two or three are gathered in my name, I am there among them.   Matthew 18.20

Some first steps

Here are some steps you can take to establish a daily time of prayer:

- *Find the time.*

- *Find the place.*

- *Plan the time.*

There is no single, 'right' way to pray that suits everyone. Some people use Bible reading notes as a framework. Others use a simple outline for prayer called a 'Daily Office'. The best guide is to discover what helps you and to use that.

There are different ways of planning a daily prayer time.

This is one way that many have found helpful.

Divide your time into three parts:

- *preparing (through praise, confession and stillness);*

- *listening (through attending to Scripture);*

- *talking (prayers on behalf of the world and yourself).*

Praying with others

The following pointers may help:

- *Keep your prayers short and to the point.*

- *Pray so that others can hear.*

- *Don't worry about how others pray.*

Give your prayers a beginning, a middle and an end and finish with 'Amen'.

Be natural and persevere. Like anything else, it gets easier with practice.

For reflection

Think about how you might develop a helpful pattern of prayer. Try to learn the Lord's Prayer by heart and pray it slowly each day, thinking carefully about the words.

Reading the Bible

Introduction

The aim of the session is to give a basic introduction to why the Scriptures are important; to give some historical background to the Old and New Testaments; and to give group members some practical ideas about how to read and study the Bible.

As with every session, adapt this one to the needs and requirements of your own group. It may be too basic for some; not basic enough for others. You may want to omit some of the historical background to the Old or New Testaments and concentrate instead on using and applying the Scriptures and listening to God through the Bible. No one can be introduced fully to Scripture in just one session: further material is available in the five-week growth course, 'Growing in the Scriptures' (in *Growth Book 2: Growing as a Christian*).

It would be a great help in this session if you could have a display of different Bibles and translations (including Hebrew and Greek, if possible) and also a selection of different Bible reading and Bible study guides for inspection, loan or purchase. You will also need a set of Bibles with the same page numbers for ease of reference.

Welcome and prayer

Welcome the group in the normal way and begin in the way you have decided in terms of prayer and worship. Recap briefly on last week's session and introduce the subject for today, possibly drawing on your own experience and practice.

The Bible and you

Ask people to reflect on their experience of prayer since the last session. Have they made any changes in their routine of prayer? Did they find this easy or difficult? The small groups should then move on to look at their experience of the Bible around the following questions:

Share in small groups your own experience of reading the Bible:

- *How much have you read?*

- *How often do you read it?*

- *Have you found it easy or hard to understand?*

- *What questions do you have about the Bible?*

Why is the Bible special?

You have to establish first that the Bible is special and then draw out why. That is where the small exhibition comes in. You may be able to use posters or a video here. Try your local library or Religious Education Resources Centre.

Looking up the Bible verses and jotting down an answer together in twos or threes will help the group disover the Bible's own testimony about itself.

Reading the Old Testament

Many Christians, new and more experienced, have great difficulty understanding and reading the Old Testament. That is why it is worth the trouble now giving them a more detailed introduction to this section of the Bible. You may feel less confident introducing it than you would be introducing the New Testament, and this section may need more advance reading and preparation than most.

A simple history lesson

This is meant to be fun – a way of sharing ignorance rather than knowledge, but also a means of giving perspective on biblical history. People should always be asked to do this exercise in groups, not as individuals. You may want to draw the time line on a very large piece of paper stuck on the wall.

Telling the Old Testament story

The time line can also be used as an introduction to telling the story of the Old Testament around the characters and events of Abraham, Moses and the Exodus, David and the Exile, which will be useful to many new Christians.

Reading the New Testament

A similar section to the one above, it helps to describe the genesis of the New Testament in the order in which it was probably written down:

1 Jesus himself did not write anything, nor did his first disciples immediately after the resurrection.

2 The letters were the first part of the New Testament to be written down. The apostles founded churches; they could not easily revisit them (because of transport) and therefore wrote to encourage them, to teach and correct the new Christians.

3 As the generation of disciples who had known Jesus began to grow older, their teachings about Jesus, which had been given by word of mouth, began to be written down in different church centres in different parts of the Roman Empire and became what we know as the four Gospels.

4 Acts was written by the author of Luke's Gospel, telling the story of the early Church.

5 Revelation was the last part of the New Testament to be written and is the hardest part to understand.

Buzz groups and plenary

After all the input, it is worth having a good time in small groups digesting what has been said and defining questions. At what seems like the right time, draw the small groups together into an open discussion and plenary.

How to read the Bible

This is a time for simple, practical guidance, some of which is printed in the Members' Handout. Members of the group can share things that have helped them.

Prayer and worship

This is an ideal session in which to have a meditation on Scripture: either a single verse or an imaginative reflection on a Gospel passage. Taking the group through Jesus' visit to the home of Mary and Martha can be a good way of drawing together the lessons of the last two weeks.

Reading for leaders

The introductory articles and charts in the *Lion Handbook to the Bible* are an excellent resource. See also *Travelling Well*, chapter 4, 'Exploring the Scriptures' and the *Emmaus* growth course: 'Growing in the Scriptures' in *Growth Book 2: Growing as a Christian.*

Summary and example timings

	mins
Welcome and introduction	5
The Bible and you (exercise)	10
Why is the Bible special?	10
Reading the Old Testament	5
A simple history lesson	10
Telling the Old Testament story	10
Reading the New Testament	10
Buzz groups and plenary	10
How to read the Bible	10
Prayer and worship	10
Coffee	

Reading the Bible

Why is the Bible special?

■ *The Bible is the world's number one best-seller each year.*

■ *This book has been translated into more languages than any other book in history.*

■ *Millions of Christians the world over come to the Bible each week and each day in church services, in small groups and on their own.*

■ *The Bible's teachings about God and humanity lie at the root of our entire civilization.*

■ *Christians believe that, through this book, God has spoken to us in a unique way and, through this book, he still speaks to us today.*

Look up these verses in small groups and write down what each one is saying about the Bible:

■ *2 Timothy 3.16*

■ *Psalm 1.1-3*

■ *Psalm 119.105*

■ *Ephesians 6.17.*

Reading the Old Testament

The Old Testament is a library of books written and collected over more than 1,000 years (the equivalent of a selection of English literature from William the Conqueror until now).

Many of the books were collected and added to gradually over this period.

The Old Testament is written mainly in Hebrew (with a little Aramaic). As a whole, the Old Testament tells the story of the nation of Israel and God's relationship with the nation.

The different sorts of books in the library need to be read in different ways. You will need help to understand the Old Testament because of the different cultures from which it comes.

You will find the following books in the Old Testament library:

■ *Law*

■ *History*

■ *Prophecy*

■ *Songs*

■ *Wisdom.*

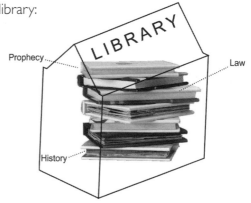

A simple history lesson

In small groups mark alongside the time line when you think the following famous people from the Bible lived, or when the events happened.

- *King David*
- *Abraham*
- *Paul*
- *Moses*
- *Jesus*
- *The Exodus from Egypt*
- *Jeremiah.*

Then, either go through the answers as a whole group, or look up the events in the time chart in your own Bible to get a sense of 2,000 years of history.

Reading the New Testament

The New Testament is a library, like the Old Testament – but with not as many sorts of books. It was written in Greek and was composed within 60 years of Jesus' death and resurrection.

The New Testament was written by Jesus' disciples and by the first generation of Christians.

The New Testament tells the story of Jesus and the early Church.

The books in the New Testament library are:

- *Four Gospels*
- *Acts (by Luke)*
- *Lots of letters (by Paul and others)*
- *Revelation.*

AD	100
	0
BC	100
	200
	300
	400
	500
	600
	700
	800
	900
	1000
	1100
	1200
	1300
	1400
	1500
	1600
	1700
	1800
	1900
	2000

How to read the Bible

Some important things to remember:

- *Read the Bible in a form you can understand – use a modern version.*
- *Don't try to read through from Genesis to Revelation.*
- *Don't use it like a lucky dip.*
- *Try to listen to what God is saying to you as you read.*

And some ways of reading:

- *Many Christians use Bible reading notes – dated or undated.*
- *Read a book of the Bible at a time for background.*
- *Use your imagination and think yourself into a passage.*
- *Meditate on a single verse.*

For reflection

Thank God for Scripture. Continue to work out your way of praying and build regular Bible reading in some form into your prayer time.

Belonging to the Church

Introduction

All new Christians, and those on their way into faith, need to learn something about what the Church is; how to belong and what their own responsibilities and expectations should be. This session is an introduction to the subject – again you can build on this in a four-session module in the growth section of *Emmaus*: 'Being Church' in *Growth Book 2: Growing as a Christian*.

There is a lot in the session. You may not be able to cover everything, but mix and match according to the needs of your own group. It is particularly important that those preparing for baptism and confirmation or other formal services of membership learn something about the denomination they are joining as well as your own local congregation, its history, priorities and vision for the next few years.

With some groups, this session will also throw up a great many questions about different beliefs and denominations and you will need to allow time for this. Clearly, as a group leader, you cannot be an expert on every subject but it may be worth reading a short summary of differences and similarities between Christian traditions, in preparation for the meeting.

Welcome and prayer

In the tradition you are now beginning to develop.

Sharing together

Ask the group to think in threes and fours about the following questions:

Share in small groups the story of your own involvement with your church.

- *What were your first impressions?*

- *What have you found helpful?*

- *What has surprised you?*

- *Have you found anything unhelpful?*

- *What would you say to the person who says 'You don't have to go to church to be a Christian'?*

This can be a very useful exercise, again allowing people to tell one another their journey to faith; and allowing them to voice what they don't like or don't understand. Allow plenty of time for the sharing and answering of questions and then draw the group together and, in plenary, ask each buzz group to summarize its discussion. You may want to write on a flip chart the different answers to the final question.

How important is it to belong to the Church?

This can be a brief input, following on from your discussion, but it should be clear. From there move people back into small discussion groups to read the picture in Acts 2.42-47 and invite them to think about these questions:

Read Luke's description of the early Church in Acts.

- *What would be attractive to you about belonging to such a group?*

- *In what ways is your church like the one described here?*

Pictures of the Church

Go through this section with the whole group. The concept of the Church is not always an easy one to grasp, even for those who have been Christians for many years. You may want to follow this section with a time for questions and responses.

Your own church

The Bible study has given you an introduction to what Christians believe about the Church. In small groups the focus now turns to the story, priorities and vision of the local church. Every Christian community has its own story. People may not know very much so, after a couple of minutes, pull the discussion back together and give some input, based around people's own answers, under the headings of 'story', 'priorities' and 'vision' of your own congregation.

How much do you know about your own local church? Share in small groups:

- *the story of your church;*

- *the priorities of your church;*

- *the vision of your church.*

Belonging to the Church

Go through the different ways of belonging to the Church briefly, talking about each in turn. A picture of concentric circles may help (there is one available in the handout for this session). Give some background and introduction to your own denomination, your congregation and the way small groups work in your church. More will be said about this later but it may help to introduce people to the idea now. Many churches are experiencing a time of significant change at the present time and it may be helpful to introduce this idea to the group.

Question time and plenary

People may have a whole range of questions. By this stage of the course it may not be necessary to draw out those questions first in small groups. Give people permission to ask about anything at all in the life and practice of the church. Field the questions as best you can.

Prayer and worship

Follow the pattern you are developing. If you are working on open prayer as a group it may help to have a few moments where people can write down prayers of thanksgiving or intercession (have pens and papers ready). Then they can either be read out by group members or by the leader. Focus particularly on prayers for the Church.

Depending on how you plan to tackle the session on Holy Communion, you may need to give some advance notice for next week's session itself and the bring and share supper.

Reading for leaders

Chapter 6 of *Travelling Well*, 'Travelling Together', will be a helpful companion to this session. The *Emmaus* growth course 'Being Church' has useful background material and supplementary handouts (*Growth Book 2: Growing as a Christian*, p. 65).

Transforming Communities by Steven Croft has four short chapters on understanding the Church, with headings corresponding to the four headings in the section 'Pictures of the Church' (in the members' handout).

There is no shortage of other good material on the nature and life of the Church. See, for example, Robert Warren, *Being Human, Being Church*; Robin Greenwood, *Transforming Church* and Michael Nazir-Ali, *The Shapes of the Church to Come*.

Summary and example timings

	mins
Welcome	5
Sharing together	10
How important is it to belong?	10
Pictures of the Church	15
Buzz groups and questions	10
Your own church	10
Belonging to the Church	10
Question time	10
Prayer and worship	10
Coffee	

Belonging to the Church

You cannot be a Christian on your own. To be a Christian means to have a special relationship with God and with other people. That relationship must be living and growing. So you need to be part of the Church if you are to grow as a Christian.

> All who believed were together and had all things in common; they would sell their possessions and goods and distribute the proceeds to all, as any had need. Day by day, as they spent much time together in the temple, they broke bread at home and ate their food with glad and generous hearts, praising God and having the goodwill of all the people. And day by day the Lord added to their number those who were being saved.
>
> Acts 2.44-47

Pictures of the Church

The early Church had no church buildings. The Church for them was a collection of people, not a place of worship. You did not just 'go' to church. You belonged to the Church and you were the Church.

The early Christians developed different images to describe this new community in relationship.

The Church in relationship with God

The Greek word for Church means 'those who are called out'. The Church consists of those who are called out by God into a new community. The Bible uses the picture of the Church as the Bride of Christ, to emphasize God's great love for the Church (Ephesians 5.25-32).

The Church in relation to herself

Christians are called to love one another (John 15.12). Together we form the body of Christ (1 Corinthians 12) – joined to one another like parts of a body and working together with our different gifts for the common good. The word 'member' originally meant 'limb'.

The Church in relation to the world

Christians are called together to be a light to the world (Matthew 5.14-15). In the power of the Spirit we are sent out to witness to God's love in our actions and our words: not to withdraw by ourselves but, like salt, to be mixed in with the whole of human society.

The Church in relation to time

Christians live in this world now as pilgrims travelling home (1 Peter 2.11). The journey is beset with danger and difficulty. We need God's grace and we need each other. One day we will reach our heavenly home and God's love will renew the earth.

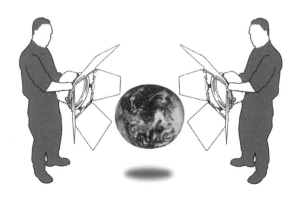

Emmaus Nurture course handout: Belonging to the Church

In the Creed we say we believe in the 'One, holy, catholic and apostolic Church'. The word 'catholic' means 'universal'. The word 'apostolic' refers to a Church built on the foundations of the apostles of Jesus and 'sent' by God with a message of love to the world.

Belonging to the Church

There are four different ways in which we belong to the Church. Each one of them is important.

1   The universal Church

The whole company of Christian believers all around the world and all through time. We are part of that great fellowship of Christians.

We are being watched, prayed for and cheered on by a great cloud of witnesses who have gone before us (Hebrews 12.1).

We have brothers and sisters in Christ all over the world today.

We are one body.

2   The denomination

We are also members of a denomination. Within the universal Church we are Anglicans or Methodists, Baptists, Roman Catholics, Pentecostals or part of some other stream.

All the denominations believe the same on the fundamentals of faith but differ on the interpretation of some things.

The denomination gives the Christian a wider sense of belonging. It lays the ground rules of belief and practice, worship, ministry and authority. But it is not enough on its own.

3   The congregation

We need to be committed members of a local church. That is our Christian family. It is where we worship every week. It is where we learn, where we care, where we move on in ministry, where we give our support financially. Belonging means being there on Sundays, giving and receiving.

4   The small group

Even congregations can be very large and relationships superficial. The quality of Christian life described in Acts 2 can often best be realized in a small group. There are different ways to do this in different churches. The important thing is to have a place where people can carry on growing, sharing and giving in a personal way.

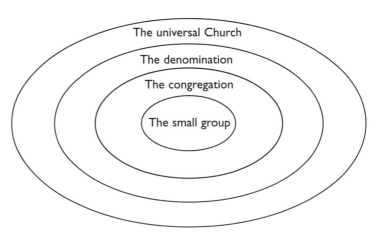

For reflection

Pray for your own church this week and think about what your own membership of the Church means (and should mean) to you.

Emmaus Nurture course handout: Belonging to the Church

Sharing Holy Communion

Introduction

There are a number of different ways of approaching this session:

- *As a straightforward teaching session about the service of Holy Communion.*

- *Combining the session with an informal celebration of Communion. This means you may need to limit the teaching element and leave people to read and think about material in the handout in the coming week.*

- *A teaching session linked with preparing for a celebration of Holy Communion the following week (which means extending your course by one session).*

The decision you take will depend on the time available in the course and also on whether you can arrange for someone who is able to celebrate Holy Communion to come and lead the session.

The outline given here follows pattern 2 (which is our preference) but two sets of timings are given at the end of the Leaders' Guide. It does help the life of the group enormously at this stage to have an evening set aside to experience worship and the service of Communion, particularly if this is combined with an opportunity to receive prayer with the laying on of hands. Please note that we have used the two names for the service interchangeably in the Leaders' Guide and Members' Handout. The term 'Eucharist' means simply 'Thank you': the whole service is our offering of praise to God. The term 'Holy Communion' describes the purpose of the service, which is meeting with God in a profound way in bread and wine.

Because *Emmaus* is intended to be used by different denominations, care has been taken to keep the language here and in the Members' Handout as simple and ecumenical as possible. The guide text for the shape of the service is *Common Worship: Order 1.* However, this is one session where you may want to add your own supplementary material.

Welcome and prayer

This follows the pattern of previous weeks (except that worship should be reserved for the Communion service). Explain the pattern of the evening to the group (you should have given notice already of what is to happen). Welcome any visitors who are to take part in the service (such as a president or musician).

Sharing together

Follow the questions given below:

What are the three most significant (or enjoyable) meals you have shared in throughout your life so far? Who were you with? What did you eat? Why was the occasion significant?

Why do we mark special occasions with special meals?

This exercise enables people to share another dimension of their story and also introduces the fundamental idea of the Holy Communion service as a shared meal.

Why do we celebrate Holy Communion?

Read 1 Corinthians 11.23-26 as an introduction to this section. Then go through the teaching input following the outline on the sheet.

Buzz groups and questions

Suggest people share in small groups for a few minutes then have a brief plenary/question and answer time.

Taking part in worship

This can be both teaching input based on the Members' Handout and a preparation for the service you are about to share. You may want to go briefly through the points on the sheet and then give a brief introduction to what is to happen.

The actions of the service

Explain briefly the structure of the Communion service. Then talk briefly about the four actions of the service. Invite the group to look through a service book together to get a sense of the overall shape of the liturgy and to look at the questions below:

In the Eucharist bread is taken, blessed, broken and shared.

Look in the service book and see what parts of the service correspond to which actions.

What do these actions mean? How do they relate to what happened to Jesus on the cross? How was his life taken and blessed and broken and shared?

How does this happen in our lives? What might it mean to call ourselves eucharistic people? People whom God is taking, blessing, breaking and using?

Preparing for worship

Depending on the group, you may like to divide them into small groups to prepare different parts of the service: the readings (which should be chosen beforehand), the songs (provide an outline with the number you need), the practical preparation (preparing the books, table, bread and wine) and the intercessions. It often works best to have a leader for each small group, who has done some advanced preparation and then to let group members decide for themselves which small group to take part in.

The Liturgy of the Word

The president should explain briefly the outline of the service and lead the group through the Ministry of the Word – possibly stopping for explanations along the way. Normally there would not be a sermon.

The Peace

Again, give an explanation of why the Peace is important and allow for an extended time of exchanging the Peace.

The Liturgy of the Sacrament

The president may want to refer to the section 'Do this in remembrance of me' to introduce that part of the service.

Clear explanation will need to be given of how people are to receive Holy Communion.

Opportunity to receive prayer

Depending on the group, it may be appropriate to offer prayer for healing, guidance, strength, renewal or any other grace from God.

Different churches and congregations will have their own practices here. One way of offering ministry is to ask people to remain standing after they have received communion if they would like prayer. The president, group leader or other minister is then able to move around the group praying in turn for each person who is standing, with laying on of hands and (if appropriate) anointing with oil. If it seems right, group members on either side of the person being prayed for can be invited to join in the laying on of hands. The whole group should be praying as each person receives ministry. It should not be necessary for the person being prayed for to have to say anything about their need – but there should be opportunity for a brief sentence or two.

Final prayers and songs

End the service with a prayer of thanksgiving and dedication. Point people forward to the next session (when Part 3 of the course begins) and draw their attention to the ideas in the Members' Handout for prayer and worship.

Coffee and supper

As the group has shared in Holy Communion together, this can also be a good evening to end with a simple bring and share supper. Inevitably this will mean people staying a little later than is normal.

Reading for leaders

Travelling Well, chapter 5, 'Food for the Journey', can be read by the group leaders and group members alongside this session. The *Emmaus* growth course, 'Growing in Worship – Understanding the Sacraments' (*Growth Book 2: Growing as a Christian*, p. 101) has a general session on worship and one on the Eucharist.

For Anglicans, the book *Common Worship Today* has a helpful guide to the *Common Worship* Communion services.

Summary and example timings

1   For a teaching session only

	mins
Welcome and prayer	5
Sharing together	10
Why do we celebrate Holy Communion?	10
Buzz groups and questions	10
Do this in remembrance of me	10
One service with many names	5
Taking part in worship	10
The actions of the service	10
Question time	10
Prayer	10
Coffee (and supper?)	

2   Teaching and Holy Communion service combined

	mins
Welcome and prayer	5
Sharing together	5
Why do we celebrate Holy Communion?	5–10
Buzz groups and questions	5–10
Taking part in worship	5
Preparing for worship	15
The Liturgy of the Word	15
The Liturgy of the Sacrament	20
Final prayers	10
Supper together	

Sharing Holy Communion

Why do we celebrate Holy Communion?

On the night before he died, Jesus shared a final meal, a Passover, with his disciples.

During the meal, Jesus gave to his disciples, for all time, this special way of remembering him: as bread is broken and shared and as wine is poured out.

We celebrate Holy Communion because Jesus commands us: 'Do this in remembrance of me.' This is the service Jesus gave us himself; it is the central act of worship of the Christian Church.

'Do this in remembrance of me ...'

The Passover is a special meal when Jews remember and re-enact the night when God set them free from slavery in Egypt. They believe that, in remembering this event in their history, the effects of it – God's salvation – will be made present today.

At the last supper, Jesus gives to his disciples a new special meal: one that remembers and makes present the greater and deeper salvation that took place when Jesus died on the cross for our sins.

Jesus gives his disciples a way of understanding and remembering his death at the centre of our worship as a sacrifice and an eternal covenant, as we share in Communion together.

The Eucharist is, therefore, an encounter with the risen Jesus. We meet Jesus in one another, because we are all members of his Body. We meet him in the words of Scripture, his living word to us. We meet him in the bread and wine, which become to us his body and blood.

As with baptism, the Eucharist is a sacrament: the outward and visible sign is the bread and wine; the inward reality is the living presence of Jesus.

One service with many names

The word **Communion** means sharing with God and with each other. The emphasis is on simplicity, community and fellowship. It is a family meal.

Eucharist means thanksgiving. In the Eucharist we give thanks for the whole of creation and for everything God has done for us in Christ. The emphasis is one of great celebration and festivity. It is a party.

The Lord's Supper refers to the service as a remembering of the last supper Jesus shared with his disciples. It reminds us of Christ's passion and death. The emphasis is one of solemnity and dignity. It is a sacrificial meal.

The Mass reminds us that Holy Communion is for a purpose. The word 'Mass' comes from the same Latin word as 'Mission'. It means 'Go!' The emphasis is on taking what we have received out into the world. It is rations for the journey.

Taking part in worship

Before the service

Plan to be there each week. Don't fit God into your spare time. Be in church in good time, ready to take part.

Prepare your mind and heart for worship and especially for receiving Holy Communion. Examine yourself. Look back over the last week. What do you need to say sorry for? What do you need to give thanks for? Who are the people you need to pray for? What help and strength do you need?

Expect to meet with God in the service, as God has promised to encounter you there.

During the service

Concentrate on what is going on. Try not to be distracted. Anchor your thoughts upon God.

Participate – join in as much as you can, with your whole heart. You're not there as a spectator but a worshipper.

Celebrate – enjoy it! Worship is about enjoying God.

After the service

Go and live it. Don't let your worship be for Sundays only. Put into practice all you have learned during the week.

Worship each day. Give praise to God seven days a week, wherever you are, whatever you are doing. Thank him for every part of your life.

A service outline

The Eucharist falls into two main halves: word and sacrament. One is about encountering Jesus in the Scriptures; the other about encountering Jesus in bread and wine.

The Preparation and Gathering

The Liturgy of the Word

- *The Creed*
- *The Prayers*
- *The Peace*

The Liturgy of the Sacrament

The Dismissal

For reflection

Buy or borrow a copy of the Communion service used in your own church. Take time this week to read through the service carefully. Think about the words and what they mean. Make a note of anything you don't understand and ask next week. Thank God each day for his gift to us of this wonderful act of worship and all it means.

part 03

Living the Christian life

Introduction

Part 3 of the Nurture course looks at five different dimensions of living as a Christian: ethics and lifestyle; ministry; work and money; relationships; and sharing the faith. Again, there is no attempt to look at every dimension of Christian living and the individual sessions themselves should be seen simply as giving a foundation or introduction to a particular subject. There are ways of going deeper in some of these areas in the *Emmaus* growth section.

By this stage of the group's life, people should know each other fairly well and the quality of the group meetings will improve and deepen quite dramatically as the end of the course approaches. Generally speaking, these five sessions have a much lower 'direct teaching' content and are much richer in exercises, discussion, working things out and sharing together. There is more Bible study in this section of the course, and it will help to have a set of Bibles with matching page numbers. Prayer and worship should continue to grow and develop in the ways you have established.

Over the last five weeks of the course you need to give careful thought to the way each person will go on growing in the weeks and months to come. The Nurture course has just been a beginning in thinking and learning about the Christian faith. There are four things to consider:

1 Will the person continue in some kind of small group. If so, which? how?

2 Would the person benefit from some kind of regular individual link with another Christian – meeting every two or three weeks for fellowship and prayer? This will partly depend on how the friendships with sponsors are building and developing.

3 How will each person make a liturgical response in a church service to the things that have been happening through the course? Is it appropriate to use some of the services of dedication, renewal or commitment?

4 Is it possible for the person to make a beginning in ministry and service in the life of the church in one form or another?

More details on how to form groups from the Nurture course are in the Introduction to the *Emmaus* course.

Because there is so much to talk about as the course comes to an end, it may well be helpful to try to see each person individually at some point over the next five weeks. A simple form based on the following table can be a useful aid in the process of helping people continue to move on.

Name	Group	Link	Liturgy	Ministry

Bear in mind when planning these times with individuals that some of the group may not yet have reached the point where they have made a commitment to Christ (and therefore will not need to be told how to go on growing). It is quite possible that some will reach the end of the course still not knowing whether or not they want to be Christians. They may be helped by further individual sessions or, possibly, by taking part in the next Nurture course.

By this stage of the course, the group may be very willing to spend a longer period of time together: a half-day or day away at a retreat centre, or even a residential (although this will need to be planned well in advance). The longer period of time could be used to cover one or more of the Nurture course sessions but could also focus on going deeper in or on another area – perhaps using the *Emmaus* growth material on Identity, Prayer or the Holy Spirit.

You will also need to begin to plan whether to have a sixteenth session: a church welcome evening hosted by the present group, which can be a stepping stone to the next Nurture course.

Living God's way

Introduction

The session is a fairly wide-ranging look at Christian ethics and lifestyle, focusing around the Summary of the Law, the third of the key texts for new Christians. The Bible study on the story of the Good Samaritan is a parallel in Part 3 to the story of the two sons in Part 1 and the parable of the Sower in Part 2. The session also explores some of the difficulty and cost of living as a Christian and looks again at words from the baptism service.

Welcome and prayer

Undertake this in the way you are developing, possibly asking other members of the group now to prepare for and open in prayer. Introduce the themes for Part 3 of the course.

The Maker's instructions

Ask people to divide into buzz groups. There may be reactions and responses to last week's session – particularly if it was a Communion service. Then ask them to look at these questions in the members' handout.

■   *In groups of three or four (and without looking) write down as many as you can of the Ten Commandments.*

■   *Of the ones you have named, which three are most often broken today?*

■   *Look up the full list in Exodus 20 and check your answers.*

Ask each group to give you their answers (before you look up Exodus 20). Then look up the commandments together and run through the list. If you can, explore the reasons behind some of the Ten Commandments (the Sabbath; do not commit adultery, etc.).

Run through the points given on the members' handout. The emphasis needs to be placed on why God gives us guidelines and instructions for life, rather than on specifics. Be sure throughout this session to emphasize the grace of God rather than the keeping of rules.

The Summary of the Law

The Summary of the Law is one of four key texts handed on to enquirers and new Christians in the *Emmaus* Nurture course (along with the Apostles' Creed, the Lord's Prayer and the Beatitudes).

Take some time to introduce the text (the version on the sheet is from *Common Worship*, p. 163). Encourage people to learn this and the other key texts by heart.

You way want to look together at the source for each of these summarized commandments (Deuteronomy 6.5 and Leviticus 19.18).

Explore together the rhythm or heartbeat of the Christian life in these two dimensions of worship (loving God) and mission (loving our neighbour as ourselves). Look at this from the perspective of a whole congregation as we come together in worship and are sent out in mission (linking back to the experience of the Eucharist) and the perspective of an individual: the call to withdraw to be with God and the call to engage in service of others.

The Good Samaritan

Explore together the parable of the Good Samaritan as the story Jesus tells to illustrate loving your neighbour as yourself. Either read the story together or watch it told on video. You may need to give some simple background about the relationship between Samaritans and Jews. Think together about the lawyer's question: who is my neighbour?

Putting it into practice

You may want to discuss each of these situations as a whole group or to give the small groups a chance to look through them first. One of the points of the different situations is to draw out a range of possible Christian responses to each situation and also to open up the idea that it is important to learn how to think in a Christian way about a whole range of different situations.

Fight valiantly!

The amount of time you give to this section may vary from group to group.

It is likely that the material covered in this section may help people to see more clearly that certain things from their past or their present lifestyle need God's forgiveness and healing. When you talk of sin it is important, therefore, to stress God's patience and grace. It may also be appropriate to mention opportunity for confession and prayer ministry. If there is time, you may want to look up these two passages where Paul describes the battle between the old self and the new:

■   *Romans 7.15-25*

■   *Galatians 5.16-24.*

Some things need spelling out in black and white for new Christians. This is your opportunity to do that. You may also find it helpful to mention (if you haven't already) cults of various kinds; involvement in unethical investments; fiddling tax returns; dishonesty at work; pornography and so on. This will need to be handled sensitively and firmly. Give people plenty of opportunity to ask questions. Again the emphasis should be on *why* these things are unhealthy or wrong and the grace of God in forgiveness and restoration rather than reading out lists of prohibited practices.

Some of the subjects you have covered (particularly in the example situations) will have increased people's sense of difficulty about living as a Christian and the way in which their faith might begin to affect every area of life. Again, it will be important to stress the grace of God in each situation and the difficulty of finding the right pathway. You may want to look back to the account of the seed that fell among thorns and in rocky places (Luke 8.6-7).

In thinking about the fight against the devil, it may be helpful to refer to the temptation narrative and to 1 Peter 5.8-9 and James 4.7. In Christian experience, we are conscious of encountering opposition not only from within ourselves and the way the world is, but also in the form of personal temptation and distraction. It is important to recognize and resist this.

It may be worth mentioning at this point that many people become Christians having been involved with all sorts of unjust and wrong practices and organizations, including involvement with the occult. Sometimes it will be easy to let go of these things. Sometimes they will have taken a dangerous grip of our lives. In those cases, there is a need for prayer and counsel and, on occasion, for what is called the ministry of deliverance: specific prayer for the release from evil. The power of Christ is both stronger and deeper than the power of any other force in the universe. Allow time for questions before moving into prayer.

Prayer

Give people the opportunity to articulate particular needs for prayer arising from the theme of the session. It may be more helpful to pray in small groups this week. If you are using *Travelling Well* as a companion to the course, refer the group to chapters 2 and 11, which pick up themes from this session. If a guided meditation would be a more helpful ending to the session, then the story of Martha and Mary (which follows the Good Samaritan in Luke 10.38-42) is a helpful way of balancing the need for a rhythm of prayer and service, worship and mission.

You may also need to give notice or opportunity for individual meetings and begin to talk about different options for people once the group comes to an end.

Reading for leaders

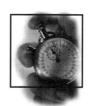

As mentioned above, *Travelling Well* has chapters on 'Being Changed' (p. 13) and on 'Times of Difficulty' (p. 109) which may be useful preparatory reading. All of the *Emmaus* growth courses in *Growth Book 3: Christian Lifestyle* are to some degree relevant to this session, especially the course on 'Overcoming Evil'.

See Robert Warren, *Being Human, Being Church*, chapter 9 for a helpful discussion of sin, using the image of gravity. The standard commentaries on Luke provide a good introduction to the Summary of the Law, the parable of the Good Samaritan and the story of Martha and Mary in Luke 10. Henry Wansbrough (*Luke: The People's Bible Commentary*) is good on all three sections.

For ways in which churches can put the parable into practice see Ann Morisy, *Beyond the Good Samaritan: community, ministry and mission*.

Summary and example timings

	mins
Welcome and prayer	5
The Maker's instructions	10
The Summary of the Law	10
The Good Samaritan	10
Putting it into practice	20
Fight valiantly!	15
Question time	10
Prayer	10
Coffee	

Living God's way

The Maker's instructions

Being a Christian is not simply a matter of what you believe. It is not simply a matter, either, of being committed to things that will help you to grow.

Being a Christian needs to affect the whole of the way we live.

God's guidelines for human behaviour are laid down in the Scriptures.

They are not to be seen as narrow rules but the Maker's instructions on how life is to be lived.

For every Christian there is a call to become more like Christ over the days and years as Christ dwells in our hearts through faith.

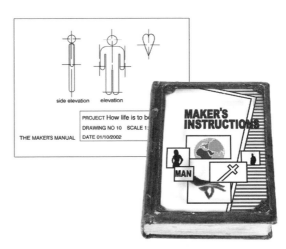

Loving God and loving others

This is the way Jesus summarized all of the Jewish law:

Our Lord Jesus Christ said:
The first commandment is this:
'Hear O Israel, the Lord our God is the only Lord.
You shall love the Lord your God with all your heart,
with all your soul, with all your mind,
and with all your strength.'

The second is this: 'Love your neighbour as yourself.'
There is no other commandment greater than these.
On these two commandments hang all the law and the prophets.

Common Worship, p. 163

Christians are called to live in this rhythm of worship and mission: loving God and loving our neighbour.

The Good Samaritan

What does it mean to love our neighbour? See the story Jesus told in Luke 10.25-37.

In the light of this story – who is my neighbour?

-     *in the place where I live?*
-     *in the place where I work?*
-     *in the context of the whole world?*

Putting it into practice

Even for Christians who are mature, it may not be always that simple to think through what is right or wrong in a situation and to put it into practice – especially when God is concerned not just for individuals but for communities and the whole world.

In small groups, take one or two of the following situations each and discuss what you would do, or what you think the Church's response should be:

■ *Diane has become a Christian recently. She has been living with her boyfriend for three years and the couple have a young daughter. Now she has become a Christian, Diane wonders what she should do about this situation. How do you advise her?*

■ *Eric works for a haulage company. He discovers that his colleagues and the works foreman are cheating the company. In the past this hasn't bothered him. Now he is a Christian, it does. How should he act?*

■ *Susan is a school governor at the local Church school. She discovers strong racist attitudes there among the governors and some of the staff in the school, which apply in the admissions policy and in the appointment of staff. What should she do?*

■ *The Church Council is reviewing the church finances for this year. A deficit is forecast of about 10 per cent of the total budget. Some members of the Council propose that the amount allocated to be given to mission and relief work be cut for that year (about ten per cent). What should the Council do?*

■ *God has given you and one or two other church members a strong burden to protect the environment. How can you make a difference in your own home, in your church and in your town?*

Fight valiantly!

It is not always easy to live as God calls us to live. The Bible tells us we will meet difficulty and opposition in the Christian life both from within ourselves and in the world around us. According to these words from the baptism service we fight on three fronts:

> Fight valiantly as a disciple of Christ against sin, the world, and the devil, and remain faithful to Christ to the end of your life. *Common Worship: Initiation Services*, p. 37

Strength for the Christian life

Perseverance is a vital Christian discipline. The continued renewal of grace to live as Christ calls us comes in large measure through the sacraments and the ministry of the Church. Receiving Holy Communion regularly, developing good disciplines of prayer and Bible reading, having the support of a group of other Christians, regularly confessing sins and seeking the ministry of healing are all ways we stay spiritually fit.

For reflection

Where is God calling you to change your lifestyle at the present time? Where do you need forgiveness and help? What strength do you need?

In the week to come, read Ephesians 6.10-20. Practise putting on the armour of God each day and standing firm in the Christian life.

Serving the Lord

Introduction

This session is about Christian ministry in its widest sense. It is largely based around two exercises: the first about church planting and mission and the second around discovering gifts and affirming one another. Both exercises not only teach valuable lessons but also help the group to develop in its life together, as group members reflect both on a task (which is imagined at this stage) and on the gifts they bring to that task.

There is no specific input in the sessions on an understanding of ordained ministry. This is because *Emmaus* is designed to be used ecumenically and the understanding of ordination varies from church to church. You may like to give your own input here or prepare supplementary material. If you do, make sure you do not detract from the main emphasis in the session, that every baptized Christian is called to live a life of service and ministry.

Welcome and prayer

Follow your normal pattern.

Into action together

Take a few minutes to set the exercise and then retire from the room with the co-leaders. It may be tempting to stay but only do this if you have one or two very difficult or vulnerable people in the group. A new dynamic will happen in the life of the group as you withdraw and the members think about a task and set goals together.

Allow plenty of time for people to decide how they will go about their task. Be sympathetic for an extension of time to 20 or 25 minutes in all. Then come back into the room and ask for a full report back. The whole exercise, and especially the reporting back, should be fairly light-hearted. Perhaps end it by asking people to say individually what they learned.

Baptism – a commission for ministry

It is important to link the theme of Christian service with that of baptism as a foundation for debunking the myth that only the ordained are commissioned for ministry. It can be a very powerful thing (especially for some enquirers) to be given a positive vision of Christian service rather than a passenger model of church membership. You may want to refer back to the commission from the baptism service (*Common Worship*, p. 170 and printed on the supplementary handout to Session 6: Becoming a Christian, page 46).

The five marks of mission

Again it is vital to help the group to an understanding of a broad concept of ministry (which embraces the whole of life) and one that is rooted in mission (rather than simply in maintaining or building up the church). The five marks of mission are a useful guide here. It may help to work through the five marks one by one, drawing out the group's understanding of what each may mean in your own local area and community. The first mark is generally seen as a 'headline' that is unpacked by the other four.

It is worth asking the group whether they would add anything to the five marks of mission or take anything away. The fifth mark was added some time after the Lambeth Conference of 1988, when the first four were agreed.

Discovering your gifts

Romans 12 is an excellent passage to explore together. You can tackle it either through a group Bible study or through a short exposition (or both).

When you have your list of gifts divide into small groups (if you have not already done so) and try to match people with gifts in as affirming a way as possible.

The end of this section would be a good place to give some input on the place of the ordained ministry within your own denomination.

Ministry now

This is meant to be a look at different opportunities for ministry.

Among ministries we are all called to exercise, make sure the group includes intercession, giving and witness. The ministries some are called to may be a very long list. It will be helpful to introduce the concept of vocation: God calls particular people with particular gifts to particular tasks.

The final question of this section is important. All too often new Christians jump into too many different things: church and doing things at church suddenly become more important than either God or their family and many problems result.

End this section with a general discussion and question and answer session.

Some pitfalls to avoid

End the session by running through the points in the Members' Handout, expanding on these where appropriate.

Prayer and worship

A re-enactment of John 13 can be very powerful given what has been shared during this session. One way to do this is to ask as many of the group as are willing to remove shoes and socks and for the leader(s) to take a towel and a basin of water, moving around the group, washing each person's feet in turn. The washing of each other's hands provides similar symbolism if the feet are one step too far!

Reading for leaders

Chapter 9 of *Travelling Well* covers similar material to this session. *Growth Book 4: Your Kingdom Come* contains an extended growth course on the kingdom, which contains material that will be helpful to those leading this session. 'Called into Life' (*Growth Book 3: Christian Lifestyle*) addresses the theme of vocation in five sessions.

Gordon Kuhrt, *An Introduction to Christian Ministry*, chapter 3, contains helpful material on baptism, service and mission. See also the foundational ecumenical document from the World Council of Churches, *Baptism, Eucharist and Ministry*. The recent Church of England report, *Called to New Life: the world of lay discipleship* is helpful on service through the whole of life.

For more on ordained ministry see Steven Croft, *Ministry in Three Dimensions: ordination and leadership in the local church.*

Summary and example timings

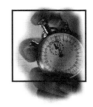

	mins
Welcome and prayer	5
Into action together	20
Baptism – a commission for ministry	10
The five marks of mission	10
Discovering your gifts	20
Ministry now	10
Some pitfalls to avoid	5
Prayer	10
Coffee	

Serving the Lord

Into action together

Imagine there is no church at all in the neighbouring community of Someplace. The members of your group are sent out by your church to plant a church in that area.

You have 15 minutes to work out how you would begin; decide what your priorities as a church are and, especially, what gifts you have in your group for ministry in the new situation.

Plant a Church

- *What are the essential tasks that need to be done?*

- *Who will exercise which ministry?*

- *Everyone must play a part in the new church.*

- *You have no premises and a grant of just £500.*

Baptism – a commission for ministry

'Those who are baptized are called to worship and serve God' (the *Common Worship* Baptism Service). Each of us needs to reflect on how we put that promise to serve into action.

In many people's minds, the Church is like a big double-decker bus. The vicar is the driver. The treasurer is the conductor. Everyone sits back and enjoys the ride to heaven. This is a very wrong picture.

A much better picture is that of a sports team. Every member of the team has a part to play. If team members don't turn up for training, the whole team suffers. If one team member switches off or doesn't bother, then the whole team is affected.

- *Every member of the team has a vital contribution to make.*

- *God has given you gifts that need to be discovered.*

- *God will call you into different ministries outside and within the Church.*

The five marks of mission

The concept of Christian ministry can easily shrink to become simply what we do in church. In fact, our Christian service is the whole of our lives offered to God in the service of the kingdom (Romans 12.1).

The Anglican Communion seeks to define Christian service in these five marks of Christian mission:

■ *to proclaim the good news of the kingdom;*

■ *to teach, nurture and baptize new believers;*

■ *to respond to human need by loving service;*

■ *to seek to transform unjust structures of society;*

■ *to strive to safeguard the integrity of creation and sustain and renew the earth.*

Discovering your gifts

In small groups, study Romans 12 together. List the different gifts that are mentioned.

Then go round your small group and attempt to say which person in your group may have which gifts in your list.

Ministry now

In small groups, or one large group, think through the different ways in which you can exercise a ministry and get involved in a ministry now.

List the number of ways in which we can be involved in ministry outside the church first (through work, home or voluntary work).

Then list the ministries within the church that we are all called upon to exercise.

Finally, list the ministries some are called to be involved in. Put an asterisk against any you are involved in already or would like to be active in.

What principles should we have for balancing our time between home, work, church and community?

Some pitfalls to avoid

■ *Your ministry is not confined to churchy things or Christian activities.*

■ *Ministry is not the sole responsibility of the clergy.*

■ *Upfront ministry is not more important than behind the scenes ministry.*

■ *'Spiritual' ministries are not more important than practical ones.*

■ *Your ministry is unique to you. Don't model yourself on anyone else.*

■ *Every form of ministry is to be undertaken as a servant.*

■ *Take time to let your ministry develop – and persevere in what you do.*

■ *A balance between prayer, rest and work is important in every Christian's life. It is easy to take on too much.*

For reflection

Think and pray during the week about your own ministry. If you are able to, use Isaiah's prayer: 'Lord, here am I; send me' (Isaiah 6.8).

Your money and your life

Introduction

This session covers three linked themes: the Christian attitude to work and vocation (which was touched on in the last session), developing a Christian attitude to money and possessions in general and, thirdly, reflections on Christian giving. Where you put the main weight of the session will depend on the needs of the particular group.

Including a session largely on money and giving may seem strange in an nurture group until you reflect on the amount of teaching Jesus gives about money in the Gospels – particularly on the way wealth is often a barrier to effective Christian discipleship. The session is also important because new Christians need to learn at an early stage of their journey about their responsibilities in giving, for their own sake and for the sake of the church to which they belong.

It may be helpful to have your church treasurer with you for the session or you could have a conversation with him or her as part of your research.

Introduction and welcome

Follow your normal pattern.

Telling your story

Ask the group to share with each other in small groups the story of their working life.

- *How old were you when you started work?*

- *What different jobs have you had?*

- *Which have you enjoyed the most?*

- *Have you had periods of being unemployed?*

- *Are you happy in what you are doing now?*

- *How has being a Christian made a difference at work?*

- *How has being a Christian changed your attitude to money?*

Be prepared to allow quite a bit of time for this one. It may be the first time the group has ever talked much about their working lives and reflected on faith and work with someone else. Be sensitive to those who are passing through hard times in employment or unemployment.

As a way of drawing the exercise together, go round the whole group and ask them to say one thing they learned or were surprised by during the time of sharing.

Christian vocation

Explain simply the meaning of vocation and draw out from the previous discussion what it may mean to live out your faith in the workplace (in terms of truth, honesty, integrity, etc.).

Ask the group if they can identify the kinds of job where Christians might fulfil their vocation and earn their living through their daily work and examples of the tent-making pattern of life. Throughout the discussion be sensitive to those who may have failed in their work or those who may not be in paid employment for different reasons.

It may help to have stories of the ways in which different people have discovered a call to a particular job and/or Christian ministry.

First principles of Christian stewardship

Explain the idea of stewardship and its deep roots in Scripture, with an emphasis, as always, on the grace of God. There will be an opportunity to explore it further in the Bible study. The concept is a significant challenge to concepts of materialism and consumerism, which are so prevalent in our society. It is wise to emphasize how radical a message this is for our society – but how much it is needed.

Bible study

This is the group's chance to prepare the church's next sermon on money. Give the small groups about ten minutes to think together about different passages and then no more than three minutes to share what they have learned with everyone else. The passages will raise significant questions, which cannot all be answered in one evening. As a whole, the exercise will stress how much teaching on money there is just in a single Gospel.

How should we give?

The second section of teaching input is based around the Members' Handout. Your own church may have some literature about ways of giving that it would be helpful to distribute and go through at this point.

Understanding your church's finances

A fairly straightforward and very worthwhile exercise, providing you have the information to hand. Aim to give the big picture rather than getting lost in a lot of figures. Place all the emphasis on faith – on God providing what is needed and on people being drawn into giving at the time and in the way that is right for them.

Steps into giving

Again be honest but avoid the hard sell. Remember especially that you will probably still have hesitant enquirers in the group who may have been put off in the past by churches that were simply after their money. Explaining the steps without any pressure is normally something people find very effective.

Ways of giving

Give essential information as efficiently as possible.

Questions

There may not be many questions this week – but it is always worth asking.

Prayer and worship

Follow your normal pattern, leading into coffee and chat.

Reading for leaders

Some of the material on ministry is relevant to vocation. Chapter 8 of *Travelling Well* may also be helpful.

On giving and stewardship see Michael Wright, *A Handbook of Christian Stewardship*; Peter Maiden, *Take my Plastic*. Church House Publishing produces a leaflet, *All things come from you*, in packs of 10 to explain basic principles of Christian stewardship.

On money generally see Keith Tondour, *Your Money and Your Life* and, on a likely pastoral issue arising from this subject, see Keith Tondour, *Escaping from Debt*.

Charles Handy is one of the most stimulating writers on the future shape of work: see *The Empty Raincoat* for an introduction to his thinking. For a substantial reflection on money, debt and our society see Peter Selby, *Grace and Mortgage: the language of faith and the debt of the world*.

Summary and example timings

	mins
Introduction and welcome	5
Telling your story	15
Christian vocation	10
First principles of Christian stewardship	10
Bible study	15
How should we give/Church finances	15
Buzz groups and questions	10
Prayer	10
Coffee	

Your money and your life

Christian vocation

In the Gospels Jesus calls people to follow him and to particular forms of service. Christians believe the risen Christ calls people to service today – the word 'vocation' means a call.

All Christians try to live out their faith in their workplace.

Some Christians fulfil their vocation and earn their living mainly through their daily work.

Some Christians earn their living through their daily work to support their calling to ministry in other ways (as St Paul made tents to support himself).

Discovering your vocation at different periods of your life is an important part of being a disciple.

First principles of Christian stewardship

All that we have comes from God. God calls us to be good stewards of all we have been given. God is concerned not simply with what we give but how we approach all we have. According to Genesis 1 and 2, our stewardship extends to caring for the whole world.

> Yours, Lord, is the greatness, the power,
> the glory, the splendour and the majesty;
> for everything in heaven and on earth is yours.
> All things come from you,
> and of your own do we give you.
>
> *Common Worship*, p. 291, from 1 Chronicles 29.11 and 14

Bible study

Each group should take one or two of the passages listed below. Read them together and draw out of them the main teaching on money and possessions.

Draw together into one group. Each group should present to the others what they have found in the passage.

- *Luke 12.13-31*
- *Luke 18.18-30*
- *Luke 19.11-27*
- *Luke 20.20-27*
- *Luke 21.1-3.*

How should we give?

God has given so much to us and asks us to be as generous in return. The New Testament instruction is to give:

- *in proportion to our income;*
- *in a regular and disciplined way;*

- *in a way that is realistic to the need;*
- *in secret;*
- *with joy.*

God is more concerned about how we give than about how much.

Tithing

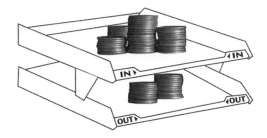

The Old Testament standard of giving was the tithe – one tenth of our income. Many Christians still give in this way. For some, giving a tenth will be something to work towards. For others it will be just a beginning.

Understanding your church's finances

Obtain some information about your church finances (from your treasurer or copies of last year's accounts).

Work out your answers to the following questions in small groups:

- *What was your total church expenditure for last year?*
- *What does that work out at each week?*
- *What are the five largest items in the budget?*
- *How much did your church give away last year?*
- *What is the budget for this year?*
- *How much was income last year?*
- *How much does that work out at each week?*
- *What proportion of income comes from the giving of church members?*
- *How much tax was reclaimed from charitable covenants?*

For discussion: How much do you think church members should be called upon to give?

Steps into giving

These are some steps people make in their giving from when they first become Christians. Don't feel pressured. Pray about your giving and talk it over with your family. God is patient with us in this area (as in every other). If the rest of your family are not Christians that will clearly affect your own giving.

- *Casual giving.*
- *Responsible giving.*
- *Proportional giving.*

For reflection

Thank God for all you have been given. Pray this week about your own attitude to money and possessions and about how much you should give. Take some practical steps once you have prayed through your decision.

Learning to love

Introduction

Leading Session 14 needs great sensitivity both to the group and to the Holy Spirit. It comes near the end for that very reason: group members are likely to be more open to each other now than they have ever been and able to talk about deeper areas of their lives – particularly their relationships.

Welcome, introduction and prayer

Follow your normal pattern.

You and yours

Again an opportunity for people to talk to one another about another dimension of their lives: the relationships within the family and with close friends.

Ask the group to share in small groups:

- *Who are the people you have been closest to in your own life?*

- *Does your list include: parents, siblings, spouse, friends and children?*

- *Why do you think so many people find these relationships so difficult?*

End the exercise by collecting together answers to the final question from the different groups and look together at the first paragraph on the Members' Handout.

Bible study

Invite the group to study 1 Corinthians 13 quietly on their own at first. Each person will need a copy of the text.

- *Read it through once as it is written.*

- *Read it through a second time substituting the name 'Jesus' for 'love'. What do you learn about Jesus?*

- *Read it through a third time, substituting your own name for 'love'. What do you learn about yourself?*

Be prepared for people to discover some uncomfortable truths about themselves as they read the passage for the third time.

Now discuss the passage in small groups. Share what you have learned about Jesus and about yourself (if you can).

- *What do you learn about love in marriage and in family life?*

- *What does the passage teach you about growing up?*

- *Which verse of the passage speaks to you most clearly?*

You will probably want to draw together the small group discussion to look at the last two or three questions.

Building good relationships/ barriers in relationships

Again, use the notes in the members' handout and expand these into your own input, or draw good lessons and principles out of the group members themselves.

What happens when things go wrong

Many of the people in your group will probably be carrying hurt from relationships that have gone wrong. Some of that hurt may be surfacing at the present time. But some, almost certainly, will stay below the surface for some time: there are so many good things happening in a new relationship with God and with other Christians. After that initial period, however, these wounds sometimes begin to surface and God begins to deal with these deeper areas of people's lives.

What you say in this section, therefore, may not apply immediately to the group, but it is essential information for them as they look ahead over the next couple of years (and in many ways to the rest of their lives) to God setting right and healing what is wrong inside.

What you are able to share will depend to some extent on your own experience of these things in yourself and in other people. Testimony, openness and vulnerability on your part will almost certainly enable the group to go deeper in its discussion and allow group members to admit to hurts and wounds in different areas of their lives at a later date. The important things to stress are the great love of God and the way in which God's work in our lives continues over many years.

Growing closer to God

You may want to end the session by looking at the way the group members are growing in their relationship with God. Again, many in the group may not have found a problem in experiencing and receiving the love of God in different ways, but some may. This is a good opportunity to share a little about the right place for emotion and feelings and sensing God's presence in prayer, worship and the whole of our Christian lives.

Buzz groups and discussion

After all the input, give people the opportunity to talk together and then draw the group together into a plenary discussion and question time. Before you bring this to a close, offer to continue the discussion afterwards on an individual basis with anyone who would find this helpful.

Prayer and worship

You may need longer for this than usual in this session. A meditation can be helpful. An opportunity for ministry may be right.

Reading for leaders

Chapter Two of *Travelling Well*, 'Being Changed', is the link chapter for this session.

The two great spiritual classics, *The Revelation of Divine Love* by Julian of Norwich and *The Imitation of Christ* by Thomas à Kempis both have a great deal of material on growing in love.

Paul Goodliff, *Care in a confused climate: pastoral care in a postmodern culture* is a good overview of the subject. The book has two chapters on creating relational health and healing the wounded soul which are relevant to this session.

The areas of relationships and healing are generally well resourced by Christian bookshops. For a readable overview see Mary Pytches, *Yesterday's Child*.

Video and multimedia material

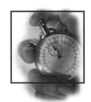

Human relationships are a continual theme of soaps and films. There will be no shortage of illustrative material on how relationships can sometimes be difficult, which will make a good starter for discussion. Choose something light or serious depending on the mood of the group.

Summary and example timings

	mins
Welcome, introduction and prayer	5
You and yours	15
Bible study	15
Building good relationships/barriers in relationships	10
What happens when things go wrong	15
Growing closer to God	10
Buzz groups and questions	10
Prayer and worship	10
Coffee	

Learning to love

You and yours

The relationships in our lives bring us the deepest joy.

They can also bring us the deepest pain we will ever know.

These joys and pains come through being a friend, a wife, a husband, a child or a parent.

As Christ begins to change our lives, and as we learn his way, so our relationships should begin to change as well.

Bible study

The world means many different things by love.

The Christian model for love in all our relationships is Jesus.

Paul sums up the new understanding of love he has come to in Jesus in his famous chapter on love, 1 Corinthians 13.

Building good relationships

Some things build good relationships between people, whether in friendship, marriage or parent–child relationships. These include:

- *quality time spent together;*
- *sharing yourself;*
- *appreciating each other (and using words to do it)*

- *listening to each other;*
- *allowing other people to be themselves;*

What others can you add to the list?

Barriers in relationships

Barriers form between people for many different reasons. These are some of the most common.

Think about them in small groups. Try to give some practical examples for each one – and write down some ideas on how to overcome them.

- *Pride*
- *Unforgiveness*
- *Fear*
- *Jealousy.*

Emmaus Nurture course handout: Learning to love

What happens when things go wrong

Many people come to Christ bearing wounds from relationships that have gone badly wrong.

Sometimes, even after you become a Christian, you will sustain serious hurt through relationships.

Christ is able to heal these inner hurts from the past and to set them right. Often, as part of our Christian growth and development, God will allow hurts from the past to come to the surface again so that they can be healed. This process is sometimes known as inner healing.

At the core of this healing is receiving forgiveness yourself for the wrong you have done and forgiving others who have wronged or hurt you very deeply.

When you forgive someone you are releasing all the pain and bitterness and anger you have carried for years against that person.

You are not saying, 'What so and so did does not matter', and you are not saying, 'What so and so did was right'. You are saying, 'What so and so did to me was wrong and hurt me very deeply. But in Jesus' name I forgive them anyway.'

To forgive is like cleansing a wound – all the infection goes and, over the weeks and months, the wound is then able to heal instead of remaining open and festering.

The healed failure, the forgiven sin, become the place where Christ's power rests upon us like a tent pitched over our weakness (2 Corinthians 12.9). The thickened scar tissue is stronger than the original, undamaged flesh.

> Though healed, the soul's wounds are still seen by God, not as wounds but as honourable scars… Our courteous Lord does not want his servants to despair even if they fall frequently and grievously. Our falling does not stop his loving. Peace and love are always at work in us, but we are not always in peace and love. But he wants us this way to realise that he is the foundation of the whole of our life in love and furthermore he is our eternal protector and mighty defender.
>
> Julian of Norwich, *Revelations of Divine Love*, chapter 39

Growing closer to God

Growing as a Christian is about coming to love God more and coming to realize more and more deeply how much God loves you.

Share together in small groups:

- *Are there any people you realize you need to forgive?*

- *How will you go about that?*

- *How easy do you find it to believe that God loves you?*

For reflection

Thank the Lord each day for those close to you and build up a habit of praying for them by name. Invite the Lord to show you any areas of your life where you need to forgive or that need healing.

Sharing the faith

Introduction

The aim of this session is to enable the members of the group to look back over what they have experienced through the *Emmaus* Nurture course and forward to a lifetime of Christian discipleship. The session is structured around two Bible passages. The fourth key text in Christian nurture is passed on in the study of the Beatitudes. The text is a portrait of Christian character, ministry and mission for the kingdom and is therefore an appropriate way of drawing together Part 3 of the course (in the same way as the Apostles' Creed draws together the material in Part 2). The second passage is the story of the Emmaus road, which forms a way of helping people to reflect on their own experience of their journey to faith and ways in which they might share their faith with others.

You will need some space in the session for looking at what is to happen after the group ends, based on the decisions you have made in individual meetings with people over the last few weeks. You may need to plan the welcome evening together (a process that is about helping this group to grow, as well as drawing others to faith). You may also want to celebrate the end of the course with a party or by going out for a meal together.

Welcome, prayer and introduction

Follow your normal pattern.

Sharing together

Ask people to divide into small groups and tell the story of their journey through *Emmaus* over the last 15 weeks or so. They should focus on the questions:

- *What has been most significant and helpful for you?*

- *Where do you still need to grow?*

Once people have talked to one another for a few minutes, go around the room inviting each person to say something to the whole group (you may still need to give one or two people permission to pass).

The Beatitudes

The translation given of the Beatitudes is identical to *Common Worship* (p. 164) and follows the English Language Liturgical Consultation (ELLC) translation.

Introduce the text either from the members' handout or from the Bible. Set a context for the Beatitudes in Scripture and in the Sermon on the Mount. You may want to say a little about the meaning of each saying, taking care to show how relevant each beatitude is for all of us.

It may help to ask the group to think about these questions:

- *What strikes you most?*

- *What puzzles you most?*

- *What gives you most hope?*

- *What do the Beatitudes leave you wanting to discover/do?*

The end and the beginning: sharing the journey of faith

Ask the group to read the story of the Emmaus road in Luke 24.13-35 and think together about the questions on the members' handout, which invite the group first to think about these three elements in the story, then to reflect on these elements in their own experience and, finally, to reflect on how they might find a place in their own witness to the faith.

How do we share our faith?

These points may emerge naturally from the Bible study on the Emmaus road story. If they do not, you may want to highlight them now.

End the session with a final opportunity for questions.

Where do we go from here?

At the end of the evening there may be some decisions to take or notices to be given about how the group moves on from here.

If the group is to move on to engage with the *Emmaus* growth material, you should have some idea about where you might begin from the group's engagement with different themes over the last few weeks.

Reading for leaders

Chapter 10 of *Travelling Well* is on the theme of 'Christian Witness' and can be read by leaders and members of the group alongside this session. There is an extended *Emmaus* growth course on the Beatitudes in *Growth Book 4: Your Kingdom Come*. This session draws on some of the material in the first session of that course.

The first of the *Emmaus* Bible Resources, *The Lord is Risen!*, aims to help individuals, groups and congregations to explore Luke 24 as a whole. See especially chapter 4, 'Eyes Opened', on the Emmaus road story and evangelism.

Robert Warren's book, *Living Well* (the Archbishop of Canterbury's Lent Book for 1999) is a study of the Beatitudes.

Summary and example timings

	mins
Welcome, prayer and introduction	5
Sharing together	15
The Beatitudes	15
The end and the beginning	15
How do we share our faith?	10
Buzz groups and questions	10
Where do we go from here?	10
Prayer	10
Coffee	

Sharing the faith

The Beatitudes

The teaching of Jesus in the Sermon on the Mount in Matthew's Gospel is introduced with these eight great promises of blessing. Together they describe the character of Christ and the character of Christ's people.

Blessed are the poor in spirit,
for theirs is the kingdom of heaven.

Blessed are those who mourn,
for they will be comforted.

Blessed are the meek,
for they will inherit the earth.

Blessed are those who hunger and thirst for righteousness,
for they will be filled.

Blessed are the merciful,
for they will receive mercy.

Blessed are the pure in heart,
for they will see God.

Blessed are the peacemakers,
for they will be called children of God.

Blessed are those who are persecuted for righteousness' sake,
for theirs is the kingdom of heaven.

Matthew 5.3-10

Each beatitude begins with good news of God's grace. Each contains a surprising character trait not valued by the world. Each ends with a particular gift from God.

Each beatitude is for all of us. Some are principally about our attitude to ourselves or to God. Others are about our attitude to God's world and about sharing in God's mission today.

The Beatitudes are about the present and the future: the people we are and the people God is calling us to be and giving us grace to become.

The end and the beginning: sharing the journey of faith

Look together at the story of the Emmaus road and the way in which the risen Jesus draws alongside two disciples who are moving in the wrong direction.

In the story there is:

- *a time when Jesus draws alongside and listens;*

- *a time when Jesus teaches;*

- *a time when Jesus reveals himself in a new way.*

Can you find these three elements in the story?

Can you find each of these elements in your own journey of faith?

What lessons can you draw from this story about how to share your own faith with others?

How do we share our faith?

Through prayer

How will you pray regularly for your family and friends?

Through our lifestyle

We are all ambassadors for Christ in the way we live. Jesus calls us to be servants to one another and to those around us.

Through what we say

If we are praying, and if our lifestyle is right, we may be given natural opportunities to share our faith. Often the best way to witness in words is to tell the story of how you became a Christian.

Through pointing people to others

Often we may not feel we have the words, or that we are very good at explaining what we believe. But we can lend a book or a tape that has helped us; we can invite people to special events and services; we can give people some idea of where to look if they want to find out more.

For reflection

Thank God for all you have received through this *Emmaus* Nurture course. Begin to pray regularly for your family and friends that their eyes may be opened to know the risen Christ.

part 04]

Additional resources

A welcome evening

The format for this should be very simple.

- *Plan the date for a few weeks after the Nurture course ends and a few weeks before the next course is due to begin.*

- *Produce simple invitations in advance.*

- *Distribute invitations through the existing group, through church services, through contacts with families bringing children to baptism and couples coming to be married, and through the network of the congregation. People should be encouraged to come with their friends rather than send them.*

- *The existing nurture group should provide a good-quality simple supper.*

On the night, welcome people informally and provide a drink as they arrive. When most people have gathered give a more formal welcome and outline the plan for the evening. Say grace and serve the supper.

When everyone has eaten give a very short and lively presentation about the Christian faith – possibly including a couple of short testimonies from the existing group. Talk briefly about the next course: about what happens, where it is held, the kind of material covered and when it begins. Have printed invitations available.

Leave plenty of time at the end of the evening for coffee and more drinks and for talking to people informally.

Sponsors on the way of faith

Why have sponsors?

One of the best ways of welcoming and befriending those who are beginning the way of faith is to give them a sponsor. This helps people feel part of a community of faith. Relationships are developed not just between the enquirer and the person leading the nurture groups, often the priest or minister, but with an individual member of the church. Because the group will be made up of several enquirers and several sponsors, the nurture group itself becomes a microcosm of church. Seekers and committed Christians explore and share faith together. In this way the sponsor embodies the welcome, friendship and loving concern of the whole congregation.

The nurture stage of *Emmaus* will work well without sponsors, but many dimensions of people's journey into faith will be immeasurably strengthened if the church develops this ministry.

When do the sponsors take up their role?

The nurture stage is in three parts. The sponsor can be appointed either straight away to accompany the person all the way through, or at the end of Part 1, where the enquirer makes a decision to go forward towards initiation. If the sponsors are to be part of the nurture group, it is probably best that at least some potential sponsors are present from Session 1 – even if they are not linked with enquirers until Part 2. Otherwise the whole process of group building would need to begin again.

What do sponsors actually do?

Emmaus is an accompanied journey. The role of the sponsor is to be a companion on the road for those who are enquiring about the Christian faith. Some churches have chosen to call the sponsors 'companions' (which means someone who shares bread with us) because of the other meanings of the term sponsor in modern English.

In the terms of the *Emmaus* story, the sponsor is called to be Christ for that person. This is a big responsibility, but it is also a tremendous joy and privilege. The sponsor is not expected to have all the answers to the many questions that are bound to arise, but the sponsor is expected to be a faithful, praying member of the church. This means being committed to pray regularly for one's companion and to be open to sharing experiences of faith. The sponsor will, therefore, usually take a full part in the nurture groups. As friendship grows, it is hoped that the sponsor will encourage and help deepen the faith of the person they are sponsoring, but the chief commitments are to attend the meetings, to prayer and to being a friendly contact within the life of the church. This clearly needs to involve some contact outside of church services and meetings, but this side of the ministry needs to be allowed to develop naturally. There can be nothing worse for both the sponsor and their candidate than for the church to try to impose close, personal friendship upon them. If it develops, that is all to the good. If it doesn't, the primary role of the sponsor is not diminished.

There is also a public aspect to being a sponsor. At the different services that mark stages of the way of faith the sponsor accompanies the candidate. Here the sponsor represents the church bringing new people to Jesus.

Who could be a sponsor?

In theory, any baptized member of the church can be a sponsor. In practice it is often best to choose someone who, it is felt, will get on well with the person they are sponsoring. Often there will already be an existing friendship that can be built on. In many cases the reason someone is taking part in a nurture course is because of the witness of a member of the church, which arose out of friendship. In these cases it will be obvious who should be the sponsor. Sometimes it will not be clear. And sometimes a close friend will seem quite the wrong person to choose. There is no reason to shy away from appointing a stranger to be the sponsor. You are not actually making these people become close friends, but offering the friendship of Christ through the ministry of another Christian. Provided the person who is going to be the sponsor understands his or her role, is diligent in prayer, open to sharing faith and prepared to make the necessary commitment, this is very often the best way forward.

Different churches will want to develop different policies for how to provide this ministry. Many churches have, over a period of years, sought to involve virtually the whole congregation. This is enormously enriching. By taking part in a nurture course the sponsors have their faith strengthened and renewed. It is in giving that we receive. Most people who act as sponsors discover it to be a most rewarding ministry.

Who appoints the sponsor?

This will be the role of the clergy and those leading the nurture course. However, common sense dictates that those on the way of faith are consulted where appropriate to make sure the candidates themselves understand why they are being given a sponsor and that they are happy about the person the church is appointing.

How long does the commitment last?

Officially, the role of the sponsor ends with the baptism or other service of initiation by which the candidate becomes a full member of the Church. However, the way of faith is very concerned with keeping those who come to faith and helping that faith to grow to maturity. Although there is no official role for the sponsor in the growth stage of *Emmaus*, it is hoped that the friendship and prayerful concern that has begun will continue in one way or another, perhaps through an ongoing one-to-one link.

One of the biggest reasons people lapse from faith is not a loss of faith itself, but because people do not feel valued or cared for within the Christian community. The natural friendships and the loving relationships that build up through the companionship of sponsors and new Christians can be one of the best ways of encouraging this care for one another. If the church is also developing lay models of leadership and pastoral care, possibly within the growth groups or courses, then the new Christian who comes to faith through *Emmaus* will have the best possible chance to grow to maturity.

On the following pages are a handout to be photocopied or adapted and given to potential sponsors in the congregation, and an outline meeting for a preparation meeting for those who want to take on this ministry.

Sponsors on the way of faith

What is the way of faith?

Emmaus: The Way of Faith is a means of welcoming people into the Christian faith and the life of the Church. It understands that, for most people, coming to faith is a long process.

The *Emmaus* course provides the church with materials and resources for building relationships with those outside the church and accompanying enquirers on their journey of faith.

However, the most important resource is people. We believe that meeting people where they are, listening to their concerns and sharing experiences, is crucial if we are to accompany people who are searching for truth. Feeling that you are valued and that you belong often comes before knowing you believe.

This is what Jesus did on the Emmaus road (Luke 24.13-35). He walked with those two disciples, even while they were heading in the wrong direction. He listened to them, and he shared with them the truth of the gospel.

What is a sponsor?

A sponsor is someone who is appointed by the church to be a companion to someone who is enquiring about the Christian faith. The sponsor embodies the care and concern of the whole church.

What is involved?

A sponsor would normally accompany an enquirer to all the meetings of the *Emmaus* Nurture course where the basics of a Christian faith and life are explored. The sponsor does not lead the meetings, but joins in as an ordinary group member. A sponsor is not expected to know all the answers, but a sponsor does need to be willing to share his or her own experiences of being a Christian. This will involve the sharing of difficulty and doubt as well as comfort and joy.

The sponsor will also pray regularly for the candidate; visit the candidate from time to time in their home; be a point of contact for that person when they come to church services and take part in the different services that mark the stages of the journey towards commitment and full membership.

Being a sponsor is an enormous privilege. We represent Christ to others, meeting them on the road of their life at a crossroads of decision. Most of the people on the Nurture course will not yet be Christians. They will just be starting that process of turning to Christ. They will have many questions. The sponsor will try to be a loving companion and a living signpost directing the way to Christ.

Who could be a sponsor?

This ministry is open to any baptized member of the Church. The requirements are openness to God, sensitivity to others and a commitment to offer prayer and support. This is something any faithful Christian could do. It is about having a loving heart not an eloquent tongue!

We may not think we have the spiritual resources for this ministry, but actually we all have something to share and something to contribute to the journey of faith. First of all we are on the journey ourselves. We all have a story to tell of how we became a Christian. We all have experiences of God. We all struggle to make sense of life.

Please consider offering yourself as a sponsor on the way of faith. Even if you feel that this ministry is not for you, please pray for those who are enquiring about the Christian faith that, as a church, we may faithfully accompany these people as they journey to God.

Emmaus Nurture course handout: Sponsors on the way of faith

Preparation meeting for sponsors

Before the meeting make sure that people have seen the handout on sponsors.

The aim of this meeting is to:

1   explain the *Emmaus* model for accompanying people to faith;

2   explain the role of the sponsor;

3   begin the process of understanding and sharing our own experiences of God.

Some or all of the material here will be useful in a preparation meeting for sponsors. The Bible study on the *Emmaus* road may also be useful in other preparation meetings for your church, where you are discussing using the way of faith.

The meeting for sponsors should be led by a group of people, including the priest, vicar or minister and those who are to lead the nurture stage of *Emmaus*. It may be helpful to have one or two people there who have themselves acted as sponsors, to talk briefly about their own experience and answer any questions.

1 *Emmaus: The Way of Faith* – Bible study and feedback

Read the story of the Emmaus road in St Luke's Gospel (Luke 24.13-35) and in small groups (if there are more than six people it is best to split up) ask these questions:

- Why don't the two disciples recognize Jesus?

- What is Jesus' attitude to them?

- What makes them recognize Jesus?

- What is their new attitude to him?

- What does this story tell us about mission?

After about 15 minutes get the group(s) to report back.

Emphasize the following points. Many of these may already have emerged.

- Jesus conceals his identity because he wants people to make a free choice to know him, love him and serve him.

- Jesus listens before he speaks. His first words to them are 'What is it you are talking about as you walk along?'

- Eventually Jesus is recognized. But this is at the end of a long journey. On that journey people have shared their experiences and insights and Jesus has explained to them the true meaning of the Scripture. The moment of recognition itself involves their eyes being opened to see things as they really are.

- The two disciples are filled with joy and long to share with others the truth they have received.

- This story teaches us that coming to faith is like a journey. The journey has different stages. It involves listening as well as speaking, exploring as well as explaining.

■ The *Emmaus* material provides a framework for ordering the Church's mission around these insights. In particular, it provides a nurture course for those who want to explore the Christian faith. We call these people enquirers. When they have come to a decision to become members of the Church we shall call them candidates.

2 Sponsoring someone on the way of faith

A sponsor is appointed by the church to be a companion to someone who is enquiring about the Christian faith. The sponsor embodies the care and concern of the whole church.

Go through the sheet 'Sponsors on the way of faith', explaining the various points and providing opportunity for discussion. If it is a large group you may like to put people back into their smaller groups and ask them to come up with any questions they want to ask.

The most important points are these:

■ *Anyone can become a sponsor. No special qualifications are required.*

■ *A sponsor is not expected to know all the answers.*

■ *A sponsor is expected to:*

  ■ *share their faith*

  ■ *offer friendship*

  ■ *pray regularly.*

3 Sharing faith

The *Emmaus* model rests on the idea of an accompanied journey. People will find it easier to come to faith and to stay as part of the Church if they build good relationships with other Christians. This will be about sharing faith as part of Christian friendship.

We all have experiences to share.

Ask people to turn to their neighbour and tell them the story of how they became a Christian. Give people five or ten minutes to share their stories.

After this has happened it may be useful to point out that most people did not share stories of sudden conversions (though this may be the experience of one or two). Most will share a story of a process and of key people along the way who encouraged their faith and accompanied them on their journey. This can be demonstrated by a simple show of hands. If you want to go into this more deeply, John Finney's books *Finding Faith Today* and *Stories of Faith* outline stories and statistics of people's faith journeys.

Now ask people to think of the biggest barrier that gets in the way of their continuing journey of faith, and the source of their biggest encouragement. Invite people to share these experiences in pairs or in small groups of three or four. We are not trying to give answers here but hope to encourage mutual support and sharing of experience. It is this that will be the biggest contribution sponsors make to the nurture group process.

4   Prayer

Ask people to write down on one piece of paper a single word to sum up their biggest barrier to prayer and, on another piece of paper, a single word to sum up their biggest encouragement.

First of all place the 'barriers' around a lighted candle. This can be done either in silence or with a short petition from each person. Then place the 'encouragement' over someone else's 'barrier'. It is by sharing and by mutual support that we overcome the obstacles in our path and grow together into maturity of faith.

Read again the *Emmaus* story from verse 28.

Have a time for open prayer if that seems appropriate.

Ask people to pray for each other as they decide whether being a sponsor is the right thing for them.

Share the Peace together.

Summary and example timings

	mins
Welcome, prayer and introduction	5
Bible study and feedback	25
Sponsoring someone on the way of faith	20
Sharing faith	20
Prayer	20

Resources for worship and prayer

As with any journey, so with the way of faith; there are different stages to pass through. As people grow in their faith it can be important and helpful to mark and celebrate these different stages with the whole Christian community. The services suggested here are celebrations of a growing commitment to Jesus Christ. At the heart of this commitment will be the main service of initiation: baptism and confirmation, or for those who have already received these sacraments but have lapsed, a reaffirmation of their baptismal faith.

For this edition of the *Emmaus* Nurture course we have revised and simplified the services we offer in the light of experience, building on the most recent thinking of the Church of England's Liturgical Commission (which builds in turn on experience around the Anglican Communion and in other Churches). A set of suggested resources was published by the Commission in 1998 to complement the new Initiation Services. In consultation with members of the Liturgical Commission we have developed these further in the text here and provided these and other resources on the CD-ROM. For those who wish to use and develop the different set of services in the first edition of Nurture, you will also find the text of these on the CD-ROM.

In this edition we have not reproduced the main service of Baptism, Confirmation or Affirmation of Baptismal Faith from the Initiation Services, although for your convenience we have included the texts from this service again in the wider resources on the CD-ROM. This service (or the equivalent one in your own church), used in an appropriate way for each candidate, will normally form the main public response and recognition for what is taking place in each person's journey.

The services here should therefore be seen as supplementary material which may be helpful in building closer links between the life of the nurture group and the worshipping life of the congregation. Three services are provided:

1   *Welcoming an Enquirer in the Way of Christ.*
     For use in public worship after the first part of a nurture group.

2   *Evening Prayer for a Nurture Group.*
     For regular use during the later part of a nurture group as a framework for prayer.

3   *A Service of Welcome after Baptism, Confirmation or Affirmation of Baptismal Faith.*
     For use when candidates have been baptized, confirmed, received from another church or have affirmed their baptismal faith in a different church (as, for example, at a deanery confirmation service). This service is adapted from that provided in the first edition of the Emmaus Nurture courses.

You are welcome to make copies of the text for local use. The full text of the services is included on the CD-ROM together with the following supplementary material:

■   prayers with learners in the Way of Christ (from GS Misc 530);

■   services for the presentation of the four texts (adapted from GS Misc 530).

We envisage these materials might be used as part of the prayer life of the nurture groups themselves and from time to time in Sunday worship, for example, in the intercessions following a service in which enquirers have been welcomed.

1   Welcoming an enquirer in the way of Christ

The service normally takes place after the Liturgy of the Word and should be held at or near the font.

Minister   Today it is our joy and privilege to welcome N and N
                 as disciples in the way of Christ.

*The minister invites the enquirer(s) to come and stand before the people. They and their sponsor(s)
come forward. The sponsor may introduce them by name.*

The following Affirmation of the Christian Way may be used

Minister   As we follow the way of Christ,
                 we affirm his presence among us.

Voice 1   God calls us to learn the way of worship.

Voice 2   Jesus said:
                 Where two or three are gathered in my name,
                 I am there among them.
                 Jesus, you are the way: meet us in the way.

Voice 1   God calls us to learn the way of prayer.

Voice 2   Jesus said: Remain in me, and I in you.
                 Jesus, you are the way: meet us in the way.

Voice 1   God calls us to learn the way of Scripture.

Voice 2   Jesus met his disciples on the road
                 and opened the Scriptures to them.
                 Jesus, you are the way: meet us in the way.

Voice 1   God calls us to learn the way of service.

Voice 2   Jesus said of those who served the needy:
                 As you did it to the least of these, you did it to me.
                 Jesus, you are the way: meet us in the way.

The minister says

                 (N and N/Friends,)
                 We thank God for his presence in your life/lives
                 and for the grace that has brought you here today.
                 We welcome you.
                 What is it that you seek?

Enquirers   To learn the way of Christ.

Minister	Jesus has opened for us the way to the Father.
All	**Seek and you will find.** **Knock, and the door will be opened to you.**

Minister	God of life, guide N and N by your wisdom and surround *them* with your love. Deepen *their* knowledge and love of Christ and set *their* feet on the way that leads to life. May your people uphold *them* in love, find in *them* a sign of hope, and learn with *them* the way of Christ.
All	**Amen.**

The minister may pray in silence or in his/her own words with each enquirer. The candidate is handed a copy of the Scriptures or of a Gospel with the following words

Seek in this book new life in Christ,
who is the Word of God and the hope of the world.

The minister may address the sponsors

As we have welcomed N and N/these enquirers,
so will you accompany them on the journey of faith,
supporting them with friendship, love and prayer?

All	**With the help of God, we will.**

The minister addresses the congregation

People of God,
we have welcomed N and N/these enquirers
in the love and hope of Christ.
Will you support and pray for them,
and learn with them the way of Christ?

All	**With the help of God, we will.**

The service continues with the prayers of intercession and the Peace.

2   Evening prayer for a nurture group

Preparation

The Lord almighty grant us a quiet night and a perfect end.
Amen.

Our help is in the name of the Lord
who made heaven and earth.

A period of silence for reflection on the past day and on the group meeting may follow.

Most merciful God,
we confess to you
before the whole company of heaven and one another,
that we have sinned in thought, word and deed
and in what we have failed to do.
Forgive us our sins,
heal us by your Spirit
and raise us to new life in Christ. Amen.

O God, make speed to save us.
O Lord, make haste to help us.

Glory to the Father and to the Son
and to the Holy Spirit;
as it was in the beginning is now
and shall be for ever. Amen.
Alleluia.

A suitable song or hymn may be sung.

The Word of God

A Bible reading from the theme for this evening.

The following verses may be used as a responsory.

Minister	As we follow the way of Christ, we affirm his presence among us.
Voice 1	God calls us to learn the way of worship.
Voice 2	Jesus said: Where two or three are gathered in my name, I am there among them. **Jesus, you are the way: meet us in the way.**
Voice 1	God calls us to learn the way of prayer.
Voice 2	Jesus said: Remain in me, and I in you. **Jesus, you are the way: meet us in the way.**
Voice 1	God calls us to learn the way of scripture.
Voice 2	Jesus met his disciples on the road and opened the scriptures to them. **Jesus, you are the way: meet us in the way.**

Voice 1	God calls us to learn the way of service.
Voice 2	Jesus said of those who served the needy: As you did it to the least of these, you did it to me. **Jesus, you are the way: meet us in the way.**

Gospel Canticle: The Song of Simeon

Now, Lord, you let your servant go in peace:
your word has been fulfilled.

My own eyes have seen the salvation
which you have prepared in the sight of every people;

A light to reveal you to the nations
and the glory of your people Israel.   (*Luke 2.29-32*)

Glory to the Father and to the Son
and to the Holy Spirit;
as it was in the beginning is now
and shall be for ever. Amen.

Prayers

Intercession and thanksgivings may be offered here.

Silence may be kept.

As our Saviour has taught us, so we pray

**Our Father in heaven,
hallowed be your name,
your kingdom come,
your will be done,
on earth as in heaven.
Give us today our daily bread.
Forgive us our sins
as we forgive those who sin against us.
Lead us not into temptation
but deliver us from evil.
For the kingdom, the power,
and the glory are yours
now and for ever.
Amen.**

In peace we will lie down and sleep;

for you alone, Lord make us dwell in safety.

Abide with us, Lord Jesus,

for the night is at hand and the day is now past.

As the night watch looks for the morning,

so do we look for you, O Christ.

**The Lord bless us and watch over us;
the Lord make his face shine upon us and be gracious to us;
the Lord look kindly on us and give us peace. Amen.**

Notes

This order of service is based upon an adapted Order for Night Prayer (Compline) from *Common Worship: Daily Prayer*. It is designed to be used at the end of an evening meeting of a nurture group. With most groups it will be appropriate to introduce shared prayer at some point in the course. One possible point to do this is after Part 1, but it is important to be sensitive to the way in which the group is developing. Be particularly sensitive to the needs of those who are still enquirers.

The use of a pattern for prayer will not be appropriate in every setting but it may be helpful in providing a shape and words for praise, penitence and intercession whilst also leaving space for some extemporary prayers.

At the end of the evening session it may be helpful to have a short break before the prayers. You may want to rearrange the furniture and, perhaps, light a candle or introduce some other symbols of worship.

As the life of the group develops, different members may want to lead the prayers with appropriate support. In the weeks of the course which focus on the four texts the supplementary material for the Presentation of the Apostle's Creed, the Lord's Prayer, Jesus' Summary of the Law and the Beatitudes may be used instead of the Bible reading and response.

The service of Night Prayer has been adapted by including the Affirmation of the Christian Way as a response to Scripture, omitting the psalm and antiphon to the canticle for the sake of simplicity, and including the Lord's Prayer, as is appropriate for a group of enquirers and new Christians.

The order of service is designed to be photocopied onto a supplementary handout and copied for group members.

With a group which is meeting during the day, it will be possible to develop a similar order for prayer based upon Prayer During the Day in *Common Worship: Daily Prayer*.

3   A service of welcome after baptism, confirmation or affirmation of baptismal faith

For use when candidates have been baptized, confirmed, received from another church or have affirmed their baptismal faith in a different church (as, for example, at a deanery confirmation service).

After the Liturgy of the Word the newly baptized and/or confirmed and those who have renewed their baptismal promises stand before the congregation.

President   We welcome the newly confirmed [and those who have renewed their faith in Christ].

You have entered into full membership of Christ's Church. In the name of the Lord we welcome you.

Testimony by the candidates may follow.

Sponsors and others from the church offer words of welcome. All may say

> **We welcome you into the Lord's family,**
> **and into the fellowship of [name of church].**
> **May Christ strengthen you with the bread of life**
> **as you grow in his love and service**
> **and in membership of the Church.**
> **We welcome you.**

The prayers of intercession follow and include prayers for the newly baptized.

The president introduces the Peace with these or other suitable words

> God has made us one in Christ.
> He has set his seal upon us
> and, as a pledge of what is to come,
> has given the Spirit to dwell in our hearts.
>
> The peace of the Lord be always with you
> **and also with you.**

At the end of the service the president may lead the candidates and the congregation in the Commission (Initiation Services, p.170; Common Worship: Services and Prayers for the Church of England, p. 359.)

Bibliography and further reading

All things come from you, 2nd edition, Church House Publishing, 2002.

Baptism, Eucharist and Ministry, World Council of Churches, 1982.

Called to New Life: the world of lay discipleship, Church House Publishing, 1999.

Combined Mission Praise, Marshall Pickering, 1999.

Common Worship, Church House Publishing, 2000.

Common Worship: Daily Prayer, Church House Publishing, 2002.

Common Worship: Initiation Services, Church House Publishing, 1998.

Lent, Holy Week and Easter, Church House Publishing/SPCK, 1986.

On the Way: towards an integrated approach to Christian Initiation, Church House Publishing, 1994.

Alexander, Pat and David (eds), *The Lion Handbook to the Bible*, 3rd edition, Lion, 2002.

Augustine, St, *Confessions*, Everyman's Library, 2001.

Bunyan, John, *The Pilgrim's Progress*, Collins, 1960.

Church of England Doctrine Commission, *The Mystery of Salvation*, Church House Publishing, 1995.

Cottrell, Stephen, *Praying through Life*, National Society/Church House Publishing, 1998.

Cottrell, Stephen and Croft, Steven, *Travelling Well: a companion guide to the Christian faith*, Church House Publishing, 2000.

Croft, Steven, *Ministry in Three Dimensions*, Darton, Longman and Todd, 1999.

Croft, Steven, *The Lord is Risen!*, Church House Publishing, 2001.

Croft, Steven, *Transforming Communities*, Darton, Longman and Todd, 2002.

Day, David, *Pearl beyond Price*, Fount, 2001.

Earey, Mark and Myers, Gilly (eds), *Common Worship Today*, HarperCollins, 2001.

Finney, John, *Finding Faith Today*, British and Foreign Bible Society, 1992.

Finney, John, *Stories of Faith*, British and Foreign Bible Society, 1995.

Goodliff, Paul, *Care in a Confused Climate*, Darton, Longman and Todd, 1998.

Green, Michael, *Baptism*, Hodder and Stoughton, 1999.

Green, Michael, *I Believe in the Holy Spirit*, Hodder and Stoughton, 1998.

Green, Michael, *The Day Death Died*, Darton, Longman and Todd, 1982.

Greenwood, Robin, *Transforming Church*, SPCK, 2002.

Handy, Charles, *The Empty Raincoat*, Arrow, 1995.

Julian of Norwich, *Julian of Norwich – a revelation of love*, Arthur James, 1996.

Kirk, J. Andrew, *What is Mission?*, Darton, Longman and Todd, 1999.

Kuhrt, Gordon W., *An Introduction to Christian Ministry*, Church House Publishing, 2000.

Maiden, Peter, *Take my Plastic*, OM Publishing, 1998.

Morisy, Ann, *Beyond the Good Samaritan: community, ministry and mission*, Mowbray, 1997.

Nazir-Ali, Michael, *The Shapes of the Church to Come*, Kingsway, 2001.

Nouwen, Henri, *The Return of the Prodigal Son*, Darton, Longman and Todd, 1997.

Pritchard, John, *Learning to Pray*, SPCK, 2002.

Pytches, David, *Come, Holy Spirit*, Hodder and Stoughton, 1995.

Pytches, Mary, *Yesterday's Child*, Hodder and Stoughton, 1996.

Ramsey, Arthur Michael, *Be Still and Know*, Collins/Faith Press, 1982.

Ramsey, Arthur Michael, *Introducing the Christian Faith*, SCM Press, 1961.

Selby, Peter, *Grace and Mortgage: the language of faith and the debt of the world*, Darton, Longman and Todd, 1997.

Stott, John, *The Cross of Christ*, Inter Varsity Press, 1989.

Thomas à Kempis, *The Imitation of Christ*, St Pauls, 1993.

Tondeur, Keith, *Escaping from Debt*, Sovereign Word, 1998.

Tondeur, Keith, *Your Money and Your Life*, SPCK, 1996.

Wansbrough, Henry, *Luke: People's Bible Commentary*, Bible Reading Fellowship, 1998.

Warren, Robert, *An Affair of the Heart*, Highland Books, 1999.

Warren, Robert, *Being Human, Being Church*, Marshall Pickering, 1995.

Warren, Robert, *Living Well*, Fount, 1998.

Wilkinson, David, *God, Time and Stephen Hawkins*, Monarch, 2001.

Wright, Michael, *A Handbook of Christian Stewardship*, Mowbray, 1992.

Wright, Tom, *Luke for Everyone*, SPCK, 2001.

Other resources referred to in the text

Jesus, Genesis Project Production by Inspirational Films, directed by Peter Sykes and Jon Kirsh.

Jesus of Nazareth, 1977, video by Carlton Visual Entertainment.

The Star Wars Series, video by 20th Century Fox Home Entertainment.

The Simpsons – Heaven and Hell, directed by David Silverman and Klay Hall, Fox.

The Truman Show, 1998, video by Paramount Home Entertainment, 1999.

'The Christ we share', 2nd edition, set of postcards from USPG/CMS and the Methodist Church.

'The Return of the Prodigal Son', postcards and posters from Pauline Books and Media, Middle Green, Slough SL3 6BS. Web site: www.pauline-uk.org

The authors

Stephen Cottrell is a residentiary Canon of Peterborough Cathedral. Until recently he was a member of the Springboard Team and is a former Wakefield Diocesan Missioner. He is editor and co-author of *Follow Me*, a programme of Christian nurture based on the catechumenate, which is widely used by Anglo-Catholic churches. He has also written *Praying through Life*.

Steven Croft has been the Warden of Cranmer Hall within St John's College, Durham, since 1996. He was the Vicar of Ovenden in Halifax for nine years. He is also the author of the handbooks *Growing New Christians* and *Making New Disciples*, and his work has pioneered understanding of the relationship between evangelism and nurture. His recent work includes *Ministry in Three Dimensions: Ordination and Leadership in the Local Church* and *Transforming Communities: re-imagining the Church for the 21st Century*.

John Finney was, until 2002, the Bishop of Pontefract and was also the Decade of Evangelism Officer for the Church of England. His report *Finding Faith Today* has been instrumental in helping the Church understand how people become Christians. He was also involved in the writing of *On the Way – Towards an Integrated Approach to Christian Initiation* for General Synod.

Felicity Lawson is Vicar of St Peter Gildersome in the Diocese of Wakefield and is a former Dean of Ministry and Diocesan Director of Ordinands in that diocese. Together with John Finney, she wrote *Saints Alive!*, a nurture course helping Christians towards a deeper understanding of life in the Spirit.

Robert Warren was Team Rector of one of the largest and fastest growing churches in England, St Thomas Crookes. He succeeded John Finney as the Church of England's National Officer for Evangelism and is now a full-time member of the Springboard Team. His book *Building Missionary Congregations* sees the catechumenate as one of the potential ways for facilitating the change required as we move from inherited patterns of church life towards the emerging models that will shape the Church in the next millennium.

Although all five authors are Anglicans, the *Emmaus* material can be used by any denomination and has been produced with this in mind.

Using the CD-ROM

Running the CD-ROM

Windows PC users:

The CD-ROM should start automatically. If you need to start the application manually, click on *Start* and select *Run*, then type **d:\nurture.exe** (where **d** is the letter of your CD-ROM drive) and click on OK. The menu that appears gives you access to all the resources on the CD. No software is installed on to your computer.

Mac users:

Use the Finder to locate the resources in the folders described below. The menu application will not work on a Mac, but you will still be able to access the resources.

Viruses

We have checked the CD-ROM for viruses throughout its creation. However, you are advised to run your own virus-checking software over the CD-ROM before using it. Church House Publishing and The Archbishops' Council accept no responsibility for damage or loss of data on your systems, however caused.

Copyright

The material on the CD-ROM is copyright © The Archbishops' Council 2003, unless otherwise specified. All industry trademarks are acknowledged. You are free to use this material within your own church or group, but the material must not be further distributed in any form without written permission from Church House Publishing. When using images or resources from the CD-ROM please include the appropriate copyright notice.

Handouts

The written resources require *Adobe Acrobat Reader* for display and printing. If *Acrobat Reader* is already installed on your computer, it will be loaded automatically whenever required. If you do not have it, you can install *Acrobat Reader* from the program within the **acrobat** folder on the CD, or by downloading the Reader from www.adobe.com.

Acrobat files cannot be edited. If you want to change the content of one of the resources before printing it, locate the document in the **rtf** folder on the CD. This folder contains files in *Rich Text Format* that can be read by most word processors. Copy the document to your computer and remove its read-only setting before opening it with your word processor.

Graphics

The cartoons and images can be loaded into your own image editing software for resizing and printing. The files are within a folder called **images** on the CD. The CD includes both high and low resolution images; the low resolution images will be more suitable for older computer systems.

The hi-res images are in the TIFF format and are suitable for printing, projection and OHP acetates. The low-res images are in the JPEG format and are more suitable for web pages and other applications where high quality definition is not essential.

You can edit the JPEG and TIFF files with most image software. Remember that the image on the CD is 'read only'. If you want to edit the image, you should first copy it to your computer and remove its read-only attribute.

For Windows users, selecting an image from the thumbnails displayed by the menu application will prompt you to copy the image before opening it. If you select 'yes', the image is copied to a Emmaus Nurture folder within your My Documents folder on your PC and the read-only attribute is removed automatically. The location of your My Documents folder varies from PC to PC but should be available as an icon on your desktop. On Windows 95 systems that predate Microsoft's use of My Documents folders, the Emmaus Nurture folder will be created on your c:\ drive.

On the CD is an image browser called IrfanView. This is free for non-commercial use (see www.irfanview.com) and can be used to view the images and perform basic editing tasks such as resizing. It runs under most versions of Windows. Please note that Church House Publishing accepts no responsibility for the use of this third-party software nor can we provide support for its use.

Error messages

You may receive the error message, 'There is no application associated with the given file name extension.' If you are trying to read one of the handouts, you should install the Adobe Acrobat Reader and try again. The same error may also be displayed if you are trying to read one of the RTF documents (from the **rtf** folder) and your word processor is unable to read this format. If you are opening one of the image files, your system does not have any software registered for use with JPEG or TIFF files. Install the free copy of IrfanView and during its installation make sure you associate .TIF and .JPG extensions with IrfanView.

PowerPoint presentation

The CD-ROM contains presentations on Emmaus Nurture using Microsoft's PowerPoint. This will enable you to present the key facts about the course to groups within your church.

If you have PowerPoint 97 or later installed on your computer, you can use it to run the presentation directly from the CD. The presentations are in named folders within the **ppt** folder on the CD. If you do not have PowerPoint, install the free viewer **PPView97.exe** from the **ppt** folder itself.

If the text in the presentation is poorly displayed, use the version of the presentation called pngsetup.exe. This will copy the presentation to your PC, complete with embedded fonts.

Links

The links to web sites require an active Internet connection. Please ensure you can browse the web before selecting an external web site. We accept no responsibility for the content of sites not produced by Church House Publishing.

Further help

If you experience problems with the CD, please visit the Nurture section of the Emmaus web site at www.e-mmaus.org.uk. We will post further help or support issues on this site.

Emmaus: The Way of Faith

If you have enjoyed using *Nurture*, you may be interested in the other *Emmaus: The Way of Faith* material. This resource is aimed at adults and is designed to help churches welcome people into the Christian faith and the life of the Church. It is rooted in an understanding of evangelism, nurture and discipleship that is modelled on the example of Jesus, as portrayed in the story of the Emmaus road.

Emmaus has three stages: **contact, nurture** and **growth**. It begins by encouraging the vision of the local church for evangelism and giving practical advice on how to develop **contact** with those outside the Church. The course material provided includes this 15-week **nurture** course that covers the basics of the Christian life and four **growth** books that offer Christians an opportunity to deepen their understanding of Christian living and discipleship.

Emmaus: The Way of Faith Introduction: 2nd edition
£4.95   0 7151 4963 6
Essential background to both the theology and practice of *Emmaus* and includes material on how to run the course in your own church.

Leading an Emmaus Group
£5.95   0 7151 4905 9
Straightforward and direct guide to leading both Nurture and Growth groups. It lays a biblical framework for group leadership, using Jesus as the example and model.

Contact: 2nd Edition
£6.95   ISBN   0 7151 4995 4
Explores ways that your church can be involved in evangelism and outreach and make contact with those outside the Church.

Nurture: 2nd Edition
£22.50   0 7151 4994 6
A 15-session course covering the basics of Christian life and faith.

Growth: Knowing God
£17.50   0 7151 4875 3
Four short courses for growing Christians: Living the Gospel; Knowing the Father; Knowing Jesus; and Come, Holy Spirit.

Growth: Growing as a Christian
£17.50   0 7151 4876 1
Five short courses for growing Christians: Growing in Prayer; Growing in the Scriptures; Being Church; Growing in Worship; and Life, Death and Christian Hope.

Growth: Christian Lifestyle
£15.00   0 7151 4877 X
Four short courses for growing Christians: Living Images; Overcoming Evil; Personal Identity; and Called into Life.

Growth: Your Kingdom Come
£15.00   0 7151 4904 0
This Growth book looks in depth at two main issues, the Beatitudes and the Kingdom

Youth Emmaus
£19.95   0 7151 4988 1
Aimed specifically at young people aged 11–16, Youth Emmaus tackles the basics of the Christian faith.

Emmaus Bible Resources – Ideal for small groups!

Finding a middle ground between daily Bible notes and weighty commentaries, the series adopts the Emmaus approach of combining sound theology and good educational practice with a commitment to equip the whole Church for mission.

Each book contains leader's guidelines, short prayers or meditations, a commentary, discussion questions and practical 'follow-on' activities.

The Lord is Risen!: Luke 24
Steven Croft
£7.95   0 7151 4971 7
The 50 days from Easter to Pentecost are a unique period in the history of the Christian faith. *The Lord is Risen!* takes us on a journey through Luke that strenghthens, challenges, deepens and renews our Christian discipleship. An ideal 'Easter' book.

Missionary Journeys, Missionary Church: Acts 13–20
Steven Croft
£7.95   0 7151 4972 5
The book of Acts is the most exciting and dramatic in the New Testament. Throughout Christian history, men and women have returned to the book of Acts to find their faith and ministry renewed and rekindled.

A Rebellious Prophet: Jonah
Joy Tetley
£7.95   0 7151 4986 5
Prejudiced, petulant, resentful, sulky: Jonah was not just a reluctant spokesman for God, he was also a disobedient one. The story of Jonah shows how God calls and uses those who are far from perfect. As Christians, we are not all called to be prophets. But we are all called to respond in some way to God's prompting. This study of the book of Jonah challenges us to do just that.

Christ our Life: Colossians
David Day
£7.95   0 7151 4987 3
The letter to the Colossians was written to a church dominated by powerful forces and alternative spiritualities. It is thus remarkably relevant to our day. Paul's theme is no less relevant – Christ shall have first place in everything.

David Day's book encourages us to consider how to give Christ pre-eminence in every area of our lives, both personal and corporate.

Related titles

Travelling Well
A Companion Guide to the Christian Faith
Stephen Cottrell and Steven Croft
£6.95   0 7151 4935 0
Provides instruction for important areas in Christian life such as prayer, reading the Bible, worship and relating faith to daily life. Ideal for adult Christians who are beginning the journey of faith.

FOOTNOTE
If you would like to receive regular updates please join the *Emmaus* database.

Send your details to
Emmaus, Church House Publishing,
Great Smith Street, London, SW1P 3NZ,
email emmaus@c-of-e.org.uk or call 020 7898 1451.

The Emmaus website: www.e-mmaus.org.uk